Sermons on the
LORD'S PRAYER

*By Ministers in the Reformed and
Christian Reformed Churches*

Edited by
HENRY J. KUIPER
Editor, THE BANNER

ZONDERVAN PUBLISHING HOUSE
GRAND RAPIDS, MICHIGAN

CONTRIBUTORS

Rev. H. Wm. Pyle, Minister of Central Reformed Church in Paterson, New Jersey.

Rev. Henry Baker, Minister of Harderwyk Christian Reformed Church, Holland, Michigan.

Rev. John Dolfin, deceased.

Rev. Wm. H. Rutgers, Minister of Kelloggsville Christian Reformed Church, Grand Rapids, Michigan.

Rev. Henry J. Evenhouse, Director of Missions of the Christian Reformed Church, Grand Rapids, Michigan.

Rev. Lubbertus Oostendorp, Minister of Graafschap Christian Reformed Church, Holland, Michigan.

Rev. Richard Oudersluys, Professor of Greek at the Western Theological Seminary, Holland, Michigan.

Rev. Martin M. Monsma, Professor of Practical Theology, Calvin Seminary, Grand Rapids, Michigan.

CONTENTS

XLV

Forty-Fifth Lord's Day

PRAYER
REV. H. WM. PYLE, TH.M., D.D.

Scripture Reading: I Thess. 5:17-18.

FOR MANY centuries instruction in the Christian religion has centered around the Apostles' Creed, the Ten Commandments and the Lord's Prayer. The Creed sums up that which the Christian must believe for his salvation; and so it is proper that it should be considered in the second division of the Heidelberg Catechism, where we are instructed as to how we are to be delivered from all our sins and miseries. The Ten Commandments and the Lord's Prayer are rightly discussed in the third division, which speaks of our gratitude for salvation. The observance of prayer, as well as obedience to the moral law, is an expression of thanksgiving to God for His redemptive work.

It may be well for us to devote a paragraph to the consideration of what prayer really is. The dictionary defines prayer as an act of worship, "the offering of adoration, confession, supplication, and thanksgiving to the Supreme Being." Bible dictionaries are more to the point. Davis says, "Prayer is communion with God. It implies that God is a person, able and willing to hear us, who has created the universe and still preserves and governs all his creatures and all their actions." Prayer is the fellowship of the creature with the Creator. For the Christian, prayer is the fellowship and communion of a child with his Heavenly Father.

If these statements are correct—and we believe that they are—then we readily see that many people entertain religious and non-religious conceptions which make it impossible for them to believe in prayer. Many have accepted a materialistic philosophy of the universe, which makes this whole thing futile. Materialists, Humanists and Pantheists have no need of this word "prayer" in their vocabulary except as they wish to speak disparagingly of the Christian's worship and supplication. In order to believe in prayer we must have the Christian conception of God. We must think of Him as a Divine Being and of ourselves as being made in His own image and likeness. The Christian believes that God is capable of hearing, seeing, speaking, feeling, knowing and willing. Long ago the Psalmist said:

"He that planted the ear, shall he not hear?
He that formed the eye, shall he not see?" (Ps. 94:9).

The Psalmist argues that a deaf God could not have made a hearing man, and a sightless God could not have made a seeing man. We may carry this deduction still further. He who gave us the power of speech is able to speak to us. He who created our emotional life can be stirred in His own heart. He who endowed us with minds to know, possesses all knowledge Himself. And He who made our wills has a perfect will of His own. We believe that God is a personal God and therefore we have no difficulty in believing in prayer, in communion and fellowship between the human person and the Divine Being.

Let us consider why prayer is necessary. The writer of the Heidelberg Catechism was not the first man to ask this question, nor the last. I have no doubt that it had been put to him frequently before he wrote it in the Catechism. Children coming to our religious education classes ask the question. Scholars in Sunday school have put it to their teachers. Adults in our church discussion groups reveal by their statements that they are still puzzled by it. They have argued that God already knows our needs and that as a loving heavenly Father He will provide for us without our petitioning for it. David said:

"For there is not a word in my tongue,
But, lo, O Lord, thou knowest it altogether" (Ps. 139:4).

Jesus said, "Your heavenly Father knoweth that ye have need of all these things" (Matt. 6:32). Since God already knows what I need, why should I pray? In my self-will, in my ignorance, in my inability to see what the future holds, I might ask for a number of things which would be very harmful to me. Might it not be better for me not to pray at all? Earthly parents make provision for their children in so far as they are able to do so, without any request on the part of the children. Will God do less than that? When our children repeatedly ask for certain things they desire, we tell them that we know what is good for them and that they ought to trust us to care for their needs. Would not silence be better than prayer and patient waiting better than repeated petitioning? And since God makes no mistakes in planning for us, is it not folly on our part to come to Him with our requests? God has said, "My counsel shall stand, and I will do all my pleasure" (Isa. 46:10). Is God going to be moved to a certain course of action in answer to the prayers of an individual, a congregation, or a nation? Since God's thoughts are not our thoughts and His ways are not our ways — but infinitely higher, better and wiser — would it not be harmful to us if He did alter His plans in answer to our supplications?

Now, you will notice that all these questions arise only in the mind of a Christian. Such questions are never asked by a pagan, for he does not entertain these high conceptions of God. The heathen thinks of God as a capricious individual who can be moved to a larger measure of mercy and love by the humble pleadings of man. He thinks of God as one who does not fully know the human heart nor understand human needs, and so must be informed. But all the questions which we Christians have asked in regard to the necessity of prayer have arisen out of the highest and the noblest thought of God. The biblical conception of God is that "He is eternal, incomprehensible, invisible, immutable, infinite, almighty, perfectly wise, just, good, and the overflowing fountain of all good." That view of God creates these questions.

It must also be observed that our incompetent and mistaken views of prayer are to some extent the cause of the question in regard to the necessity of prayer. Praying is more than petitioning. A real prayer includes also adoration, confession and thanksgiving. And, certainly, praying is not dictating to God what He ought to do. Even Christ did not do that. He prayed that the cup might pass from Him but added: "Nevertheless, not as I will, but as thou wilt" (Matt. 26:39). And the followers of Christ dare not pray in any other spirit.

All of this is further explained in the Heidelberg Catechism (Q. 116): "Why is prayer necessary for

Christians?" The answer in substance is: Because God requires it of us. He wants man to call upon Him, and so when we pray, it is in direct obedience to His command. We are to seek His face. He has said, "Call upon me in the day of trouble" (Ps. 50:15). And the parable of the unjust judge was spoken by Jesus to teach men that they ought always to pray and not to faint. We are exhorted to pray without ceasing. Since we have a sympathizing High Priest we can come boldly unto the throne of grace.

If God demands of us that we pray, the neglect of this privilege is sin. I wonder how many people look upon a prayerless life as an exceedingly sinful life. Dr. J. H. Jowett says that we have called it thoughtlessness, negligence, or even apathy; but we have not called it sin. After the people of Israel had been shown their wrongdoing in asking for a king, they said to Samuel: "Pray for thy servants unto the Lord thy God, that we die not." The reply of Samuel is significant: "Forbid that I should sin against the Lord in ceasing to pray for you" (I Sam. 12:23).

In the days of Isaiah, Jehovah looked down from heaven and knew that there was no intercessor. In the sixty-fourth chapter of Isaiah there is a prayer of the prophet in which he beseeches God for mercy and for help. In confessing the sins of the people he says, "And there is none that calleth upon thy name, that stirreth up himself to take hold of thee" (Isa. 64:7). How many intercessors does God find today as He looks down upon this world from His throne of grace? We have no right to excuse ourselves on the ground that there is no particular trouble from which we are anxious to be delivered. We cannot claim exemption from this obligation because there are times when we do not feel like it. Daily prayer is a daily duty whether or not there is any special need, whether we are in the mood or not.

The second reason for the necessity of prayer, is that it is "the chief part of thankfulness." In our introduction we referred to the fact that the writer of the Heidelberg Catechism placed the Ten Commandments and the Lord's Prayer in the third division, which deals with the expression of our gratitude to God for our salvation. The entire subject is considered under the heading of thankfulness. In his Epistle to the Thessalonians the apostle Paul wrote, "In everything give thanks: for this is the will of God in Christ Jesus concerning you" (I Thess. 5:17-18).

Turn to your Bibles and go through some of the prayers that you find there. Observe to what extent they are devoted to thanksgiving. Consider some of the Psalms which speak of God's excellency and his worthiness of receiving our praises. David penned these lines:

"I will praise thee, O Lord, with my whole heart;
I will shew forth all thy marvellous works.
I will be glad and rejoice in thee;
I will sing praise to thy name, O thou most High" (Ps. 9:1-2).

In another Psalm we find this exhortation:

"Make a joyful noise unto the Lord, all ye lands.
Serve the Lord with gladness:
Come before his presence with singing.
Know ye that the Lord he is God:
It is he that hath made us, and not we ourselves;
We are his people, and the sheep of his pasture.
Enter into his gates with thanksgiving,
And into his courts with praise:
Be thankful unto him, and bless his name" (Ps. 100:1-4).

Failure to give thanks unto the Lord is severely rebuked. The great sin of Israel, during the Exodus, was that it murmured and complained that it did not have the fleshpots of Egypt, instead of praising God that it was delivered from the Egyptian taskmasters. "The wrath of God is revealed from heaven against all ungodliness and unrighteousness of men," because God has manifested himself to men that they might know His everlasting power and divinity; and "when they knew God, they glorified him not as God, neither were thankful" (Rom. 1:21). If all men are called upon to praise God, how much more, then, does this duty rest upon those who have been redeemed by the precious blood of Christ! May God save us from being like murmuring and complaining Israel.

We have previously said that the purpose of prayer is not to inform our Heavenly Father of our needs; nor is the sole purpose to obtain from Him our needs and wants. At the same time, it is one of the means which God has ordained by which we are to obtain spiritual blessings. The third reason for the necessity of prayer, as given in the Heidelberg Catechism, is that "God will give His grace and Holy Spirit to those only who with hearty sighing unceasingly beg them of Him and thank Him for them." To think of obtaining blessings from heaven by asking for them cannot be wrong. In the light of God's promises to hear us and to answer, how could we think anything else! How definite the words of Jesus are: "If a son shall ask bread of any of you that is a father, will he give him a stone? Or if he shall ask an egg, will he offer him a scorpion? If ye then, being evil, know how to give good gifts unto your children: how much more shall your heavenly Father give the Holy Spirit to them that ask him?" (Luke 11:11-13). "Whatsoever ye shall ask in my name, that will I do, that the Father may be glorified in the Son" (John 14:13).

There is a blessed list of those who have believed God's promises to hear and answer them. In answer to the petition of Joshua, the sun stood still upon Gibeon and the moon in the valley of Ajalon. In answer to the prayer of Elijah, fire fell from heaven and consumed the burnt-offering he had prepared. And after his conflict on Carmel he prayed for rain and the heavens gave rain and the earth brought forth her fruit. David was weary in his flight from Absalom and wanted a good night's sleep. He records his experience in the third Psalm:

> "I cried unto the Lord with my voice,
> And he heard me out of his holy hill.
> I laid me down and slept;
> I awaked; for the Lord sustained me."

The early Church prayed for the deliverance of Peter from the hands of Herod with the result that an angel opened the iron gates of the prison and let the disciple out. The promises of God and the experiences of others may well lead us on to a more fervent prayer life, until we can testify from our own experience that God responds to the cries of men. Then His grace will be sufficient for us and the Holy Spirit will give us strength for the tasks, the trials, the thorns and the temptations of life.

Let us now consider what the requisites of acceptable prayer are. "What belongs to such prayer as God is pleased with and will hear?" (Heid. Cat., Q. 117). These requisites must be considered. It is more than likely that some of our perplexities in regard to God's promises to hear us and answer us have their roots in our failure to remember what is required of us.

The first requirement laid down for an acceptable prayer almost astonishes us: "That from the heart we call upon the one true God only, who has revealed Himself in His Word." This seems like a superficial statement. Does not everybody know that we must pray to none but God?

> "If we have forgotten the name of our God,
> Or stretched out our hands to a strange god;
> Shall not God search this out?
> For he knoweth the secrets of the heart" (Ps. 44:20-21).

Virtually all Protestants today know before whom they ought to bow the knees. But when these questions and answers of the Catechism were written, the errors of the Roman Catholic Church were fresh in the minds of the Reformers. It was necessary to guard the people against the custom of making prayers to the saints. Erasmus denounced unsparingly the folly of invoking particular guardian saints for special purposes, such as deliverance from toothaches, or protection in sea voyages. He said that the blind devotees placed the Virgin Mary before the Son, and prayed more often to St. Peter and St. Paul than to Christ Himself. This situation explains why we have the reminder to pray to the one true God only. And to sound a warning against prayers that are made without real thought that we are addressing God, is not out of place in the Protestant churches of today.

The saints of the Old Testament prayed to Jehovah. The disciples of the New Testament were instructed to address the Father. That supplications were made to Jesus and the Holy Spirit as well as to the Father is evident from the various epistles. And it is not wrong for us to do the same thing, for Christ is the second person in the Godhead and the Holy Spirit is the third. Still, I believe we need to remember that every good and perfect gift comes from the Father. We address Him in the name of Christ. We believe that our pleadings are heard on the basis of Christ's mediatorial work. We believe that He is our Advocate with the Father and that "He ever liveth to make intercession for us." "The Spirit also helpeth our infirmities: for we know not what we should pray for as we ought: but the Spirit itself maketh intercession for us with groanings which cannot be uttered" (Rom. 8:26).

The God to whom we pray is the one who has manifested Himself in His Word. If our prayer is to be acceptable we must rightly know God. Those who believe in no other revelation of God than that which we find in nature have a prayer language that differs decidedly from that of the Christian. We can tell to what extent their knowledge of God goes, by their terminology in addressing God. According to the Scriptures, God's divinity, power and goodness are revealed in nature. And the man with only a natural religion speaks tc the "Divine Being," the "Eternal Spirit," the "Almighty One," the "Almighty Creator," the "Infinite One" and the "Everlasting Love." All these terms, if used exclusively, indicate that the true knowledge of God is lacking. The Christian addresses God as his Father, his Saviour and his Lord.

True, God has manifested Himself in nature, but He has done so more fully in His Word. Now we know the sovereign place He holds in the universe. We recognize that in all of our prayers. Our knowledge of His majesty and glory creates in us the spirit of worshipfulness and reverence. Our knowledge of His character and His attributes guides our requests. The Christian cannot ask for anything contrary to the nature of a good and a just God.

Again, we have the injunction to pray "from the heart." Jesus plainly taught this in the story of the two men who went to the temple to pray. The publican's pleadings came from his heart and he went home justified. The self-righteous man did not really pray at all. In the conversation with the woman of Samaria, Christ said, "God is a Spirit: and they that worship him must worship him in spirit and in truth" (John 4:24).

The second requirement for acceptable prayer is a humility which is born of the knowledge of our sin. It is necessary "that we right thoroughly know our need and misery, in order to humble ourselves before the face of His majesty." The Bible is not only a revelation of God, but also a revelation of man. The full knowledge of our need and misery can be obtained from the Scriptures. All other knowledge of it is only partial. The consciousness of our sinful condition has a remarkable and sanctifying influence in our devotional life. It protects us against the spirit of the arrogant Pharisee who went up to the temple to pray. It gives us that meekness and lowliness of heart that the Lord desires in His supplicants. "God resisteth the proud, but giveth grace unto the humble" (James 4:6). And frequent meditation about the suffering and death of Christ aids us in getting that true humility. Elizabeth Clephane expressed this in her great hymn on the passion and crucifixion of Christ:

> "Upon that cross of Jesus
>   Mine eye at times can see
> The very dying form of One
>   Who suffered there for me;
> And from my smitten heart with tears,
>   Two wonders I confess:
> The wonder of His glorious love
>   And my own worthlessness."

And think of the last lines of this same hymn:

> "Content to let the world go by,
>   To know no gain nor loss,
> My sinful self my only shame,
>   My glory all, the cross!"

The person who considers his own worthlessness and his sinful self will be content to let the world go by, if only he may have the assurance that God will receive his prayers and forgive his sins.

One thing more remains to be said regarding the requisites of our supplications. We must believe God's promises to us and "be firmly assured that, notwithstanding we are unworthy of it, He will, for the sake of Christ our Lord, certainly hear our prayer as He has promised us in His Word."

Prayer is communion and fellowship with God. The disobedience of Adam and Eve in Eden shows how sin immediately breaks that fellowship. Centuries later Isaiah said to Israel: "Behold, the Lord's hand is not shortened, that it cannot save; neither his ear heavy, that it cannot hear: But your iniquities have separated between you and your God, and your sins have hid his face from you, that he will not hear" (Isa. 59:1-2). It is because of sin that man has no right to approach the throne of grace in his own name.

But Christ has opened the way for us. "We have an advocate with the Father, Jesus Christ the righteous"

(I John 2:1). From childhood we have been taught to ask God to hear us "for Jesus' sake." And we remember the words of our Lord spoken during His passion: "At that day ye shall ask in my name: and I say not unto you, that I will pray the Father for you; For the Father himself loveth you, because ye have loved me, and have believed that I came out from God" (John 16:26-27). It is because we come in the name of our advocate and our great High Priest that we have the boldness to approach the Mercy Seat.

In spite of our own unworthiness we believe that God will hear us, "as He has promised us in His Word." These promises are very definite. "Ask, and it shall be given you; seek, and ye shall find; knock, and it shall be opened unto you: For every one that asketh receiveth; and he that seeketh findeth; and to him that knocketh it shall be opened" (Matt. 7:7-8). "If two of you shall agree on earth as touching any thing that they shall ask, it shall be done for them of my Father which is in heaven" (Matt. 18:19). It is therefore in Christ that we have our confidence as well as our boldness as we bow before the great white throne.

Having considered the necessity and the requisites of prayer, we now turn our attention to the subject matter of prayer. Since God has commanded us to pray we also want to know what He has commanded us to pray for: "What has God commanded us to ask of Him?" (Heid. Cat. Q. 118). The answer of the Catechism is that we are to ask for "all things necessary for soul and body, which Christ our Lord has comprised in the prayer He Himself has taught us."

How essential it is that we should receive instruction

as to contents of our prayer; for we frequently ask amiss. Neither do we always know what is involved in our petitions. This is illustrated in the request of James and John when they said to Christ, "Grant unto us that we may sit, one on thy right hand, and the other on thy left hand, in thy glory" (Mark 10:37). Jesus plainly told them that they did not know what they were asking.

Evidently the Lord saw how necessary it was for His disciples to be told what they ought to pray for. When one of His disciples came to Him asking to be taught in the school of prayer He gave His pupil a model prayer. At that time the Lord did not tell him to pray from the heart, nor to pray in His name; but He gave guidance as to the content of prayer. He knew that His disciples needed instruction regarding the subject matter of prayer. We feel confident that the Lord's Prayer was repeatedly given to the disciples until they knew it. Luke gives it in part. Matthew gives it more completely. And the circumstances under which the two evangelists give it are also different, indicating that this instruction was repeated.

Emphasis may well be laid upon the truth that we are to ask for the things that are necessary. The unnecessary things do not have to be excluded from our supplications, but the weightier matters should come first. We have made a brief reference to the fact that our knowledge of God controls the content of our prayer and that our knowledge of ourselves helps us to pray aright. If we know ourselves we shall know our needs.

Our first need is spiritual. In the model which Jesus gave for our prayers, the hallowing of God's name and the coming of His kingdom are mentioned first. Then follows the consideration of our physical need, but this does not mean that it is the more important of the two wants of man. There is one petition for the body and there are two petitions for the soul. Knowing ourselves, we humbly ask for the forgiveness of sins. Understanding that while the spirit is willing the flesh is weak, we go to Him who was "in all points tempted like as we are," lest we fall into temptation. Note how earnestly Paul prayed for the souls of his converts. He bowed his knees before the Father that these converts might be strengthened in the inward man, that Christ might dwell in their hearts through faith, that they might know the love of Christ and that they might be "filled unto all the fulness of God." Such should be our petitions for the soul.

Physical needs must likewise be brought to the Lord in prayer. God wants us to ask for daily bread. Those living in industrial centers should petition God for an opportunity to earn it. The farmer should ask for sunshine and rain, for seed and harvest. The factory worker and farmer alike are dependent upon the heavenly Father for physical strength to carry on their tasks. In times of sickness we are to ask for recovery, believing that there is power in the prayer of faith.

However, we must not enlarge upon this discussion regarding the contents of our petitions, in as much as the separate petitions of the Lord's Prayer are discussed in detail in the following questions of the Heidelberg Catechism.

May God grant that the study of this great subject will inspire us to speak more often with the Lord. Communion and fellowship with God is a great privilege given to us by the grace of Christ. He has opened the way for us to the Holy of Holies.

> "What a privilege to carry
> Everything to God in prayer.
> Oh, what peace we often forfeit,
> Oh, what needless pain we bear—
> All because we do not carry
> Everything to God in prayer."

And let the person who does not recognize prayer as a privilege at least remember that God requires it.

Let us claim the great promise of God that He will hear us when we come in the divinely-appointed way. Ever since men first began to call upon the name of the Lord they have found the promise to be true. Moses, Joshua, Samuel, David, Elijah and all the other great wrestlers with God were men of "like passions with us." They cried out of the depths of the earth and the answer came out of the heights of heaven. They looked to God and found that He was both able and willing to help them. The promises of God hold as well today as they have ever done.

When you pray, by all means be natural and sincere. Children may "say their prayers," but adults should talk to God about the things that weigh upon their hearts. Let us practice His presence and realize His nearness. Let us commune as friend with Friend. When we pour out our ardent prayers for ourselves and for others before our Father's throne, He will let us know that He has not left His place of power and authority. We are not stretching out our hands to an empty universe. God is there. His ear is inclined to hear even the faintest cry; His Father-heart is moved to help us. Let us therefore seek His companionship as we journey on to our Eternal Home. Let us look hopefully and confidently to our Heavenly Father for all that we need for body and for soul, for time and eternity. Let us calmly and patiently wait for Him to bless us.

"Commit thy way unto the Lord;
　Trust also in him; and he shall bring it to pass" (Ps. 37:5).

In the simple but beautiful words of Oliver Holden:

> "They who seek the throne of grace,
> Find that throne in every place;
> If we live a life of prayer,
> God is present everywhere.
>
> "In our sickness or our health,
> In our want or in our wealth,
> If we look to God in prayer,
> God is present everywhere.
>
> "When our earthly comforts fail,
> When the foes of life prevail,
> 'Tis the time for earnest prayer;
> God is present everywhere.
>
> "Then, my soul, in every strait
> To thy Father come and wait;
> He will answer every prayer;
> God is present everywhere."

XLVI

Forty-Sixth Lord's Day

HOW SHOULD WE CALL UPON GOD?

REV. HENRY BAKER

Scripture Reading: Matt. 6   *Text:* Luke 11:1

"HE THAT cometh to God must believe that he is, and that he is a rewarder of them that diligently seek him" (Heb. 11:6). The address of the Lord's Prayer, "Our Father who art in heaven," expresses that confidence. The Master-Teacher taught us to pray thus. It is a well-known fact that the Lord gave this prayer to His people in answer to the request of the disciples, "Lord, teach us to pray."

None could pray like Jesus, for no other person stood in the intimate relationship to the Father that Jesus did. Jesus was a Man of prayer. He knows our needs better than any other. It is therefore not surprising that the disciples desired to learn from Him what and how to pray.

We, too, must sit at the feet of Jesus and desire that He teach us the art of prayer. It is not at all unusual for God's children to repeat the petition of the disciples, "Lord, teach us to pray" (Luke 11:1).

He has taught us; and as we give thought to the prayer so dear to the child of God, it will appear both from its form and content that we have in it the Model Prayer.

The words to which we direct your attention are rich in instruction as to the *manner* in which we should draw nigh unto God.

The forty-sixth Lord's Day, which is the subject matter for our sermon, states the reasons why Jesus taught us to address God as "Our Father who art in heaven." We desire to present them in the following order: first, because in Christ we may believe Him to be our Father; second, because He would have us approach God with reverential trust; third, because we should ever pray with due respect for His Majesty.

Prayer is the highest energy of which the human heart is capable. It is the best, noblest, and most sublime act which any creature of God in earth or in heaven can perform. "It is the chief part of the thankfulness which God requires of us." Therefore anything and everything that can magnify its exercise, enrich its content, purify its form, or make it more effective in the lives of God's children, is worthy of our thoughtful consideration. A study of the Lord's Prayer will increase our admiration for and our appreciation of its beauty.

The beginning is so tender and assuring. Hardly would a mortal being have the courage to approach the everlasting, holy and righteous God and address Him as our Father if our Saviour had not given us permission to do so. We may say, "Our Father." Jesus said we *should* say, "Our Father."

The address is very simple. A more simple form cannot be found. The Lord, we know, frowned upon vain repetition of words. Any attempt to be pompous was condemned by Him. Simplicity is a mark of sincerity. He said, "In praying use not vain repetitions as the Gentiles do, for they think that they shall be heard for their much speaking." No one need envy those who are able to draw upon a large vocabulary in their address to God. Our Lord has taught us to be simple and concise in our speech when calling upon God in prayer.

If, as James Montgomery wrote,

"Prayer is the soul's sincere desire,
Unuttered or expressed,
The motion of a hidden fire
That trembles in the breast,"

the practice to enumerate the attributes of God when we pray must be repulsive to Him. There are occasions when we are required to give an account of our faith and then it is quite proper that we confess God as we know Him; but prayer is not the proper medium for such a confession. In our prayers we speak to God, and when these proceed from the heart, our use of words in our address to Him will be natural and childlike.

It will not seem strange to anyone who knows how dear the name "Father" was to Jesus that He placed this word upon our lips. Our Lord gave preference to that name above all others. In speaking of God He used it repeatedly.

The first words recorded of Him are, "Knew ye not that I must be in my Father's house?" His last words on the cross were, "Father, into thy hands I commend my spirit." In the great Intercessory Prayer of John 17, that name appears repeatedly. He was the Son of the Father in a unique sense—the only begotten Son of the Father. That unique relationship to God stands out boldly in His teaching and prayers. Ever was He conscious of it. *He* could say, "My Father."

God was His Father, but is He *our* Father too? In-

deed He is! Our Saviour has made this very clear.
It is one of the outstanding features of the instruction
given by Christ to His own that their relationship to
God is that of children to a father. God is, according
to Jesus, a gracious Father to all who believe on the
Son of God. He is His Father and also ours.

The emphasis on the Fatherhood of God is distinctly
a New Testament one. To be sure, the Old Testament
also spoke of God as a Father to Israel. We need
but mention Psalm 103 where we are told that "His
love is like a father's to His children." In Exodus 4:22,
we read: "Israel is my son, even my firstborn." The
well-known passage of Isaiah 9:6 makes mention of
"the everlasting Father." In Isaiah 63:16 we find a
prayer addressed to Jehovah, where we find the words,
"Doubtless thou art our father, though Abraham be
ignorant of us, and Israel acknowledge us not: thou,
O Lord, art our Father; our Redeemer; thy name is from
everlasting." But even though God as a Father was
not unknown to Israel, the emphasis on the Fatherhood
of God is distinctly a New Testament one.

The Old Testament emphasis is on God's righteousness, holiness and faithfulness. The Old Testament
saints stressed more than anything else God's exaltation
above the world and His unapproachable majesty. The
Old Testament believer did not stand in that intimate
relationship to God which has become the special privilege of the New Testament Christian. Although He was
acknowledged to be the Father of Israel as a nation,
we have no hint that the believer in the days prior to
the coming of our Saviour enjoyed the consciousness
of personal sonship. That joyous experience awaited
the advent of Jesus and of the Holy Spirit. It is through
the Spirit that we know ourselves to be the sons of God.

The spiritual and ethical relationship of the believer to God is an outstanding truth in the teachings of our Lord. This sonship has its basis not in creation but, rather, in our redemption through the blood of Jesus Christ. It is indeed a serious error to ascribe to Jesus, as is popular today, the teaching that all men are the sons of God because they have been created by Him and that hence all may say, "Our Father." The adoption of sons is the believer's privilege and belongs to no other.

God's Fatherhood, of which Jesus speaks in the prayer before us, is to be taken in the restricted sense as explained in the Heidelberg Catechism: "namely, that God has become our Father through Christ." This prayer is supposed to proceed from such as realize their fellowship one with another as members of a divine family and therefore say, "Our Father." By grace we have become the image-bearers of God; yea, more, we have become partakers of the life, blessedness and peace which our Father shares with His children.

This New Testament conception of the Fatherhood of God with respect to His people is an advance on that of the Old Testament. It has been individualized, made personal, in the teaching of our Lord, so that each and every child of God may say, "Our Father." No name is richer in meaning. It is the highest revelation of God. The exalted One has come near unto us through Christ Jesus "that we might receive the adoption of sons."

It must not be concluded from the address of the Model Prayer that it must be used to the exclusion of all others. The form in which we address God depends largely upon the needs which we present to God. We may appeal to Him as a God of mercy. We may

feel the need of pleading on His power and righteousness
and therefore use words which are suitable for the
occasion. No one will consider such to be improper
on the part of God's child.

The force of Christ's instruction as to how we should
pray would be weakened by assuming that God may
not be addressed in any other words than "Our Father."
No doubt Jesus had in mind to teach that—whatever
words we use in coming to God—we should always
pray as unto One who is our Father. Prayer is in ac-
cord with the spirit of Jesus' teaching only when the
relationship of a child to his father lies at the root of
our seeking His face. We must believe that He will
be a Father to all who, trusting in the redeeming
power of Jesus' blood, call upon His Name.

We may come to Him with the boldness of a child
who has the proper filial spirit. We should go to God
as we would to our best friend. We ought to approach
Him as one who sympathizes with us, loves us and will
not withhold from us any good thing.

There are fathers of whom children are afraid.
Rather than seeking their father's help, they turn to
a stranger. Fathers there are who are harsh, cruel, un-
sympathetic, and devoid of tender affection. Our Father
in heaven, however, though stern when dealing with
sin, is infinitely good, gracious, loving and affectionate.
He has revealed His great love for us in that "He
spared not his own Son." In the shadow of the cross
we raise our prayers freely to Him. In the presence
of that eternal love we pray, "Our Father."

It is probably not out of place to remind you that
two errors, of which many are guilty, should be avoided.
On the one hand, there are those who ignore the
revelation of God which presents Him as holy, right-

eous and just. To these God is a sentimental being who condones evil and remains unaffected by the sins of mankind. They lay claim to the privilege of calling upon God as their Father, apart from Calvary. We affirm that the Scriptures of the New as well as of the Old Testament maintain the unapproachable character of God for those who have not sought peace with God through our Lord Jesus Christ.

Insisting that all men may call upon God as their Father, since He is the Creator and Sustainer of all creatures, is an abuse of the address found in the Lord's Prayer. On the basis of creation and providence, He is the Father of all creatures—even the devils—but it certainly would be blasphemous to consider the latter as having the right to say, "Our Father." Jesus explicitly tells the unbelieving Jews, who declared that God was their Father (John 8:42), "If God were your Father, ye would love me"; and in the same chapter, verse 44, "Ye are of your father the devil." Jesus' use of the word "Father," in application to God, presupposes spiritual kinship between God and man. Calling upon God as our Father when this spiritual kinship does not exist is a travesty of His teaching. That this ethical relation to God exists for him who sincerely utters this prayer is clear from its contents. In it mention is made of one's interest in God's name, kingdom and will; and also of one's need of pardoning grace and deliverance from the Evil One. Only they who believe on the Lord Jesus Christ may rightly say, "Our Father."

On the other hand, there are among us those who still stand on Old Testament ground, crying to God from afar. They hesitate to believe that they who seek their life in Jesus Christ may draw nigh in the assurance that God is their Father. The love of God for penitent sinners does not thrill them. They are in a measure still blind to the "love beyond compare." They are hesitant to believe that His loving countenance beams on all who trust in Jesus Christ. Trusting and believing hearts should pray in the assurance of His condescending love: "Our Father."

II

Christ taught us to address God as our Father in order to "awaken in us, at the very beginning of our prayer, that childlike reverence and trust toward God which should be the ground of our prayer." What is more natural than reverence when we enter into the presence of God? We should not conceive of reverence as slavish fear. Such fear takes hold of men when they stand before one whose imposing dignity terrifies them. We must reverence our God but there is no need to tremble in His presence when we seek His face.

Indeed, before one who is a father, a child need not stand in terror. And there is no father like unto Him who is in the heavens. Yet it is not strange that one who knows himself to be a condemnable sinner should fear when coming face to face with the Holy One. Does not the conviction of sin move one to fear Him who is righteous and just? Indeed, but the Lord would not have us think of Him, when we pray, as one who stands ready to inflict punishment upon the transgressor. We must think of Him as a father ready to forgive the penitent, erring supplicant. The heathen cowers before his god whose wrath must be appeased. The heathen's idol is far away and very angry with his worshiper. Not so our God. In Christ Jesus His wrath against our sins has been removed. He is reconciled to us in the blood of His Son. His heart beats warmly for His own.

One may speak of sacred fear, as indicating the true nature and meaning of reverence. There ought to be in us a feeling of profound respect in the presence of God. Holy awe is quite becoming to him who is aware of the fact that God is holy and highly exalted above us. To rush into His presence without the sense of one's unworthiness and insignificance is unbecoming to a child of God. It is and remains forever the marvel of God's grace that we may call Him "Father." In the presence of such great love we feel constrained to say: "Behold, what manner of love the Father hath bestowed upon us, that we should be called the children of God." May we stand in holy awe before the great God who, though highly exalted and having no need of us, was pleased to receive us as sons and daughters into His fellowship.

Appreciation of this blessing—a blessing greater than any other—moves the heart to sincere gratitude. Earthly wealth cannot be compared with it. It is the glory of the young as well as the old; of the learned and the unlearned; of the faltering Christian and the strong in faith. The knowledge of personal sonship gives buoyancy to our spirits. It is a tonic to weary, sin-sick souls. It is the joy and comfort of all God's saints. Such love elicits our love. Shall we not love Him who so graciously loved us? This affection is implied in reverence. It is more than holy awe. Just as it may be expected that children will respond to the sacrificing love of parents, so, too, it can be taken for granted that children of God will in thankful admiration love Him who loved us first.

The Catechism teaches us that Christ would have us trust that "God will much less deny us what we ask of Him in true faith than our parents will refuse us earthly things." Have we this confidence when drawing nigh to God? Too many, when praying, have a suspicion that their prayers will remain unanswered. They know that they should make their needs known to Him. They believe that He is able to grant them what is needed. Yet they are not assured in their hearts that the Lord will give them what they ask. Such should heed the words of James 1:6: "let him ask in faith, nothing wavering. For he that wavereth is like a wave of the sea driven with the wind and tossed."

Our Saviour taught us to lay claim on the fatherly goodness, pity, and patience of God. Even as little children will go to their earthly fathers, trusting that they will receive what they ask, so we too should approach our Heavenly Father. Our trust should be firmer than theirs, for earthly fathers at their best are evil. Our Father is infinitely good and we may trust Him implicitly.

When we pray to God we do not go to a stranger, nor to one who is reluctant to hear and answer us. He knows our needs. He loves us and is more ready to answer than we are to pray. If He were not our Father we would, in view of our sin, have reason to doubt that our prayers will be granted. Not now. His Fatherhood guarantees an answer. This, of course, does not mean that we shall receive all we ask. Many things that we think we need as being essential to our happiness are injurious to us. We may indeed thank God that not all of our petitions are granted. We rejoice that our Father knows what we need and withholds all that is harmful. We always receive the things needful. We therefore should pray in the spirit of the following prayer:

> "Through Christ, O Lord, I pray thee give to me
> Not what I would, but what seems best to Thee

Of life, of health, of service, and of strength,
Until to Thy full joy I come at length."

We expect our children to believe that what we can
and may give will not be withheld from them. Children do not always understand why parents must decline
to grant their wishes. Neither do they need to understand it. They should believe that parents will give
them all that is good in so far as it is in their power
to do so. Parents ought to assure their little ones that
they may rely on this.

Children of God never have reason to doubt that He
will answer their prayers. There should be no semblance
of doubt in us as to the integrity and kindness of Him
who has said, "Ask, and it shall be given you." It is
conceivable that children have reason to doubt the willingness of their parents. Not so the children of God.
His love is unchangeable, and having given us His
Son He freely will give us all things. Our earthly
parents may be selfish and shortsighted with respect
to their children's needs. Our Heavenly Father is bound-
less in love and understands perfectly our every want.

We should not doubt God. We have no reason to
mistrust His love. He will not fail us in our need.
Let us rest in His Fatherhood.

We can, however, have this trust of which our
Catechism speaks only when we live as children of
God. By this we mean that we can expect an answer
to our prayer only when we are children of God not
merely in name but also in our behavior. Otherwise, our
"prayers will not pass through." No child that *lives*
in disobedience to his parents can expect to receive
favors from him. Neither can a child of God expect
it. Must we then make ourselves worthy? No, that is

impossible; nor is it required. It is the Lord's practice, in dealing with His children, to show that He is a God who "pitieth them that fear Him." "The loving kindness of Jehovah is from everlasting to everlasting upon them that fear Him."

In withholding from us things we desire, the Lord corrects His people and calls them back from paths of sin. Even as of old Jehovah visited Israel with want when they departed from His ways, so today the Lord often deals with His own in the discipline of His love. This does not mean that unless we live perfect lives we shall find our prayers unanswered; but rather, that only when we live as children who strive to do His will and turn to Him for forgiveness of sins committed, may we expect to receive His blessings.

III

To the words, "Our Father" are added "who art in heaven." The reasons for doing so are "that we may have no earthly thought of the heavenly majesty of God, and may expect from His almighty power all things necessary for body and soul." The gist of this explanation from the Catechism would seem to be that we should draw nigh to God with due respect for His majesty.

The Old Testament saints in exalting Jehovah were in danger of losing sight of the fact that the essence of religion is communion with God. They conceived of God mainly as the lofty One who dwells in the heavens. To be sure, they knew of God also as dwelling with those who are of a humble and contrite spirit. Yet He was to the consciousness of the believer of that day chiefly the Lord of the heavens. He was transcendently high above him.

The address, "Our Father," implies that He is very near to us. Because of this emphasis on the condescending love of God we are likely to become unduly bold in our approach to Him, not respecting the infinite distance there is between Him as Creator and us as finite creatures. The Old Testament believer respected that distance. Do we?

It is said that "familiarity breeds contempt," although it is hardly conceivable that a child of God, because of the intimate relationship that exists between him and God, would exceed the bounds of propriety in his association with God. Yet there is a danger of losing sight, in a measure at least, of the exalted nature of the Supreme Being.

Never should we entertain earthly thoughts of Him. He is our *Heavenly* Father. He belongs not to the earthly domain, but dwells in the place of eternal glory and perfection. "As the heavens are higher than the earth so are his ways higher than our ways and his thoughts higher than our thoughts."

Although Jesus stressed the intimate relationship between God and the believer He ever maintained His heavenly, exalted character. Unlike earthly fathers, God is not partial, imperfect and changeable. Our fathers are evil; our God is holy.

It is indeed comforting to know that our Lord is highly exalted. We rest not in the care of a finite creature. Earthly fathers are noticeably restricted by the limits of time and space in supplying their children with the necessities of life. They are fickle and unreliable, wrestling with sinful flesh and selfish passions. None of these human frailties belong to Him on whom we rely.

Our Father is mighty to help. He is almighty. He

has not only the will to supply our needs but also the power. "The earth is Jehovah's and the fulness thereof; the world and they that dwell therein." He has the wherewithal to grant us the things we ask. He who dwells in heaven rules over all. His counsel shall stand; His purposes shall come to pass. No power on earth can withstand His will.

We who are helpless creatures need such an one to whom we can flee. He is our only Helper and "He makes our wants His care."

Our needs are many. Each and every moment calls for His sustaining power. "The eyes of all wait upon the Lord to give them their meat in due season." No need escapes His notice, for He is in the heavens and sees all. In grief we need His comforting presence. Trials call for His upholding grace. Only His restoring hand can deliver us from disease. In darkness He must send light. Through mist and gloom He must lead the way. In death only He can be our guide.

Truly happy is the man who calls upon God as His Father who is in heaven. Men have reason to envy the child of God who can so peacefully commit himself to the Lord.

Do we pray even as Jesus taught us? If we did we would be more assured of an answer than we often are. We would not question His faithfulness and readiness to help us in our need nor doubt His good pleasure to hear us, but confidently expect all things necessary for body and soul. Then we would have power in our praying. Great things can we expect from a great God who is at the same time our loving Father!

Is He your Father in Christ? Remember that apart from Jesus He is a consuming fire. You have reason to fear Him if you have not sought peace with Him

in Christ Jesus. You may not lay claim to His Fatherhood unless you reveal the disposition of a child who
in loving obedience honors Him. Do you?

> "The tender love a father has
> For all his children dear,
> Such love the Lord bestows on them
> Who worship Him in fear."

XLVII

Forty-Seventh Lord's Day

THE BASIC PETITION OF THE LORD'S PRAYER
The late REV. JOHN DOLFIN

Scripture Reading: Isa. 6:19; Rev. 1:4-18   *Text:* Matt. 6:9

INTRODUCTION

MANY AND varied are the appellations given to the day in which we live. Among these there is one that we desire to consider briefly in connection with the subject of our present meditation. It has been said that this is a day of irreverence or lack of respect. There is, for instance, the matter of general lawlessness that marks us as a nation. More than one writer has stated that we as a nation are the most lawless among the nations of the earth; and we do not recall that anyone has undertaken to prove the contrary.

That is indeed a terrible indictment. Without compunction of conscience, statutes and ordinances are disregarded. No one seems to be concerned about losing his standing in society for these wilful transgressions. With a smile and a laugh the fine is paid. Friends reading the names of their relatives or acquaintances in the daily list of traffic transgressors simply consider it a good joke. For other common transgressions men may be. called upon to serve time; but the complaint that an ex-convict is shunned and unable to rehabilitate himself is assuredly a thing of the past. Anyone considering this matter seriously shudders with a sincere fear as to the future. He feels, in one way or another, that a change of attitude toward the law must be brought about. It is well that we should consider as an introduction to the petition we are to meditate upon, the causes for this spirit of irreverence.

We would mention as the first cause of prevailing irreverence the universal spirit of materialism that is evident everywhere. This spirit manifests itself to an alarming degree at the present time. The Psalmist cried unto his God and said, "My soul cleaveth unto the dust; quicken thou me according to my word." Who of us, when we examine ourselves as to our Christian faith and life, would not make this word of the Psalmist his own? We feel it and humbly confess it: too often in our life the natural crowds out the spiritual. Because as a people we have paid so much attention to the things material, we have lost out on the spiritual. Our prosperity which has made us the envy of the world has robbed us of our spiritual heritage. The principles of our Puritan ancestors are laughed out of court and those who agitate for law enforcement, especially with respect to the Sabbath ordinances written into the constitutions of the majority of our States, are met with the hue and cry of "Blue Laws." They are ridiculed, mocked and maligned because of their efforts—so generally and so fiercely that they soon become discouraged, and the old order of lawlessness continues undisturbed.

As a second cause of this irreverence we would mention *false egomania*—a grossly exaggerated estimation of self. Instead of thanking and praising God for His marvelous blessings man slaps himself on the back

and says, "I am a self-made man!" In the pride of a
Nebuchadnezzar he says, "Is not this the life that I
have enriched?" A self-made generation of fools find
their counterpart in the rich fool of whom God
speaks in His Word. In the light of science there is
neither fear nor wonder left in the heart of man as he
walks in the midst of all the great and wonderful works
of God. Man has made all creatures subservient to his
will. He has harnessed the great waterfalls and uses
their power as he desires. He does not feel as our
fathers felt and therefore does not confess with them
that creation is a most elegant book wherein all creatures, great and small, are as so many characters leading
us to contemplate the invisible things of God; namely,
His eternal power and Godhead.

As a third cause for the prevailing spirit of irreverence
we would point to the spirit of unbelief. Even with
those who profess to believe there is found so much
that must be designated as unbelief. In fact some have
referred to the present generation as a generation of
practical atheists. We often act and live as if there
were no God in whom we live, move and have our
being. Because we are so often unmindful of the authority of God we are not impressed by this authority
as it is represented in the powers that be. To hear
so much sinful criticising and maligning of those set
in authority over us does not foster in us the spirit of
respect for office-bearers. This is true not only in the
State but also in the Church. The same spirit is manifest
in our religion and in our civic life. We may possess
some excellent forms but there is little reality.

Something of this spirit was also evident in the days
when our Lord lived upon this earth. It manifested
itself in the religious life of Israel. The disciples of

Jesus became aware of this, especially when they saw their Master engaged in prayer. His praying was not like that of the scribes and Pharisees. They were impressed by the fact that His whole soul was in His fellowship with the Father. That's the way they wanted to pray and therefore spontaneously it sprang from their lips, "Lord, teach us to pray." And then the Lord gave His disciples that Model Prayer, which we have learned to revere as the Lord's Prayer. This prayer is very brief as to form but it is all-comprehensive as to content. When we analyze it we are struck with the fact that the petitions answer in a very beautiful way the two great commandments of the law of life. First, there are three petitions regarding God: His name, His kingdom, His will; then, three petitions regarding man's physical and religious needs: daily bread, forgiveness of sins and deliverance from the Evil One. It is our purpose at this time to meditate on — The First or Basic Petition of The Lord's Prayer.

I. THE PLACE OF THIS BASIC PETITION IN THE LORD'S PRAYER

We cannot but take cognizance of the fact that this petition occupies the first place in the Lord's Prayer. It is given this place by Him who came from the very presence of the Almighty to make Him known unto us. The whole revelation of the Almighty revolves around the Christ of God. He who knows the Christ knows the Father. You remember, I am sure, what Jesus said to Philip: "He that hath seen me hath seen the Father." It is consequently worth-while for us to examine the reason why Jesus, when teaching His disciples to pray, should first of all tell them to say: "Hallowed be thy name." Surely it is not arbitrary, nor is it merely incidental. It is not always true, for instance, that we give God the first place in the prayers we so often utter. We so often think first of our own needs, our own desires—the things *we* want. Only when we offer a studied or liturgical prayer do we begin with God Himself. Our own interests too often crowd out the thought of God and His honor. But with Jesus, the personal Word and revelation of the Father, this could not be. He always thought first of Him whose servant He had become, whose will He had come to perform, whose work He had come to do. He was so conscious of His calling at all times that He never forgot to put His Father's interest first.

The hallowing or glorifying of God's name is indeed the highest purpose of all creation. From eternity this was what the Almighty had in mind. All works of God—in nature and in grace, in creation and in re-creation—must answer to this one supreme purpose. Therefore it is not at all strange that Jesus gave this petition first place when He taught His disciples to pray. Then again, this basic petition prepares the way for the following. It is, as it were, the gateway to the presence of God. We pray for the things that are mentioned later that the granting of these may tend to the greater praise and glorification of His name. In this they really find their answer and purpose.

Not only the first place but the supreme place in the Lord's Prayer is according to the petition "Hallowed be thy name." There is indeed a greater majesty in this petition than in all the others. Here we draw very nigh to our God for He and His name are inseparable. Surely, if we are His, we love His name, we praise His name; and still we feel that these words do not adequately express what we really mean when we pray:

"Hallowed be thy name." His name is to stand alone and to stand above all other names as the object of our reverence and devotion. Here we are, as it were, face to face with the first word of the Holy Decalogue: "Thou shalt have no other gods before me." There is to be nothing and no one in our thoughts, in our recognition, in our lives to usurp the place which rightfully belongs to God and to His glory. As we thus begin to understand something of the true meaning of this petition we readily see why Jesus accorded it the supreme place in His prayer, for it is entitled to the highest place in our hearts and lives.

Finally, we notice that our Lord accords this petition the best place in His prayer for our sake. It is always an excellent thing to make a good beginning. He who begins with hallowing God's name will, in the end, be delivered from the Evil One. Our first concern must therefore be never to think, say, or do anything that will cause His name to be blasphemed on our account. Purity of thought with respect to our God is a first requisite. The meditations of our hearts should be acceptable to our God.

To foster this we should be very careful, for instance, as to what we read. We all know that the present-day market is glutted with papers, magazines and books which no Christian, worthy of the name, should consent to read. Sometimes, when we saw such literature on the sales-racks of Christian book-dealers and pharmacists, we have wondered how they squared this with their consciences. We know these same business men would refuse to be engaged in a traffic that pollutes or destroys the bodies of men and women; why then offer for sale that which makes minds and hearts unclean in the sight of God? We fear that sufficient thought or consideration has not been given to this matter by those who love the Lord and His cause. Read only that which is clean, pure, instructive and elevating, and you will enrich your mind to the praise of God. It may be said: Show me what you read and I will tell you what you are. There is more good, clean, interesting literature on the market today than anyone can ever hope to read during his lifetime. Why should anyone feed his mind with husks when he may have the finest of the wheat? From clean thoughts come clean words. The third word of the Holy Law should not be overlooked.

We have heard of seemingly good Christian men and women who, in moments of anger or provocation, use language which savors of the underworld. The Zuni Indians, among whom we, as a Church, work with the Gospel, say: "What comes over the tongue shows what is in the heart"; and they try to picture this symbolically on their pottery. That's not a bad proverb for even a Christian to remember. We all, without exception, need a watch at the door of our mouth. James said some very hard but true things about the tongue. From thoughts and words, our deeds are born. Our deeds, too, should glorify God and not lead to the blaspheming of His name. If we stop to consider this, what a vast field for meditation is open before us. The whole matter of our relation to the world, which is hostile to God, looms up before us.

Surely a child of God is to be pitied if he cannot be satisfied with all the good things that are his in Christ but must needs turn to the world and questionable things to find satisfaction and contentment. And what an example such an one sets for others! How can he utter this basic petition of the Lord's Prayer and not realize that his life is a direct denial of it? May we all think on these things as by this petition we are brought into the very presence of our God—face to face with His perfect holiness. Let us seek in every way open to us, by the grace of God, to find that which will foster the cleansing of our thoughts, words and deeds, in order that we may become agents for the hallowing of God's name.

II. The Significance of this Basic Petition of the Lord's Prayer

This ought to become evident to all when we remember that this is a *petition, a prayer,* and that in a prayer we ask for something. With respect to this first petition and also with respect to the third, "Thy will be done on earth as it is in heaven," it is very easy to forget this. It often seems that in these petitions we are merely expressing a wish, a desire of our hearts, for instance: "Oh, that God's name might be kept holy! That His will might be done on earth as it is in heaven!" But in this way these petitions cease to be real petitions. No; we are asking God for something by means of which His name is going to be hallowed. Our teachers in the Catechism understood this and therefore interpreted the meaning of this petition accordingly. You will notice that in their interpretation they begin with the word "grant": "Grant us first rightly to know thee, etc."

The question will naturally arise in the mind of anyone who seriously considers this petition of the Lord's Prayer: By whom is the name of God to be hallowed? Not for a moment are we left in the dark with respect to this. It is to be done by us—children of men—who are here upon earth. There can be no question about the correctness of this interpretation.

To be sure, the angels in heaven hallow the name of the Lord their God, calling one to the other: "Holy, Holy, Holy is the Lord God Almighty; the whole earth is full of His glory." But for this hallowing of God's name we need not pray for the simple reason that the angels who remained faithful always do it and do it spontaneously, while the angels who have become unfaithful to their God will not and cannot do it. Neither can this petition have reference to the saints, the believers who have been translated from earth to heaven; for these also serve God night and day in all perfection. Nor can this petition have reference to other creatures, for out of all nature there arises a voice of praise and glory unto God; although this glorification of God should not be confused with the conscious praise, the hallowing of God's name for which we pray in this petition.

It remains therefore to be reiterated and emphasized that we—children of men here upon earth—are concerned in this petition. And for us there are two possibilities. For the angels and saints in heaven there is only one possibility. They can and will do nothing else but hallow the name of God. For us there is the possibility of blaspheming and also the possibility of hallowing this holy name. The former is of ourselves, or, if you will, of Satan; the latter is of God and must be granted unto us. Therefore Christ Jesus lays the petition upon our lips: "Hallowed be thy name."

We should not misunderstand this petition in any way. We are not asking for holiness to be added to God's perfect holiness. That is utterly impossible. In a real sense we cannot ask anything *for* God nor can we require anything *of* God. This petition consequently does not mean: "Thy name, O Heavenly Father, be hallowed for thine own sake. Thou art great and worthy to be praised; and since this praise is being withheld from Thee, we thy children here upon earth pray *for* Thee and *of* Thee that Thou mayest receive it."

This is not what we are asking of God in this petition. No, we recognize God to be all-sufficient, blessed in Himself and needing not to be served by the hand of man. Elihu, one of the friends of Job, understood this very well when he said: "If thou art righteous, what dost thou give him? or what does he receive at thy hand?" If we are godless and wicked we do not really rob God of anything; and if we are righteous we do not give Him anything. If we should keep the whole law and transgress in nothing we would still be unprofitable servants, for we would only be doing what is required of us. In this petition we are simply asking God to grant us all we need that His name may be honored, praised and hallowed by us in a way worthy of Him and His perfect holiness.

III. The Content of this Basic Petition of the Lord's Prayer

When we study the answer of our Catechism with respect to this we find that it is very comprehensive. First, it speaks of knowing God rightly. We presume that all who are named with the name of Christ will say: "We know God; we know Him in Christ Jesus, who came to reveal Him." But if we judge rightly, by observations which we all may make, we shall have to confess that with many there is little or no progress in this knowledge; and there are reasons for this. Some appear to be indifferent; they are satisfied to know from the Holy Scriptures and from personal experience that

God is a God of grace and love. How these attributes of His are to be harmonized with others—equally true and important attributes — as those of righteousness, justice and holiness, is of little concern to them. They are not interested in this, consider it beyond their comprehension, and put forth no efforts at all to know. They live by their emotions, more than by their faith, founded upon knowledge. A simple, pious story of the marvelous conversion of a sinner holds them spellbound and brings them to tears, while a real setting forth of the beautiful and wonderful plan of salvation presented to us by God in His Holy Word leaves them cold and unmoved. In fact the very best books on theological subjects go begging for buyers and often, if purchased, go unread.

There is indeed in this respect much to be lamented. Listen to the testimony: "We love evangelical — not doctrinal — sermons." As if there ever could be an evangelical sermon without doctrine. What they mean is that they love sermons which stir their emotions but do not tax their thinking. Thinking has become a lost art with them. Verily, a preacher, to be popular and to draw the crowd, must not preach to make them think but to satisfy their feelings. In this way of course, there can be no growth in the knowledge of God, only a retrogression in Christian faith and life. There is, indeed, too much of this in the present day, and consequently we find many carried away with every wind of doctrine that blows. They are not concerned about finding God's *truth* in His revelation, but merely about hearing things that sound pleasant and soothe the desires of the heart.

There are also some who rail against knowledge saying: "We have too much of that already; what we

really need is more fervent spirituality." How little
these folks understand themselves. They do not seem
to realize that genuine piety and true spirituality are
born of knowledge and that it is just the lack of knowledge and discernment that breeds a spurious piety with
which many are deceived to their own hurt and possible
destruction.

Understand, we are not holding a brief for that cold,
dead orthodoxy that freezes and kills every vestige of
life. We abhor it with a full and perfect abhorrence.
We detest the Pharisee with his empty forms and ac-
cursed self-righteousness. But we are pleading for a
true knowledge of God as He has revealed Himself
to us in His Holy Word. To obtain this we need to
pray, "Hallowed be thy name"; and at the same time
we should diligently search the Holy Scriptures, for
these are they that testify of Him. The better we learn
to know God in the light of the Bible the more deeply
our emotions will be stirred, the healthier will be our
piety and the richer our spirituality.

We are asking God in this petition to grant us to
know Him in all His works both in nature and in
grace. Our fathers stressed this in the Confession of
Faith which they founded upon the Scriptures. They
did not want us to walk as deaf, dumb and blind
men in the midst of all the wonderful works of God
in the realm of nature. They wanted us to see the
majesty, power and wisdom of God in His mighty
works in the sun, moon and stars; in the mountains
and valleys; in the roaring of the lion and the lowing
of the cattle; in the mighty cataract and murmuring
brook; in the trees and the flowers; in the—but why
mention more? In everything they wanted us to see
the hand and hear the voice of our God that we

might tell His praise abroad. If you would come under the spell of this, visit the Planetarium in Chicago. While you sit in the dark and watch the constellations that are brought into view by a huge machine, you listen to a most interesting and instructive lecture on some phase of astronomy. How small, how infinitely small, one feels in the presence of the divine works.

But this is not all. Our fathers also wanted us to know our God in His goodness, righteousness, mercy and truth as revealed in His marvelous works of re-creation. Not Satan but God—our God—is going to triumph. We do not deny that there is a real danger of losing ourselves in the works of God and thereby robbing ourselves of God Himself. It seems so difficult for us to keep the right balance; therefore we pray that God will grant us to know Him in all His works. We do not want the works without Him, who is their author. On the other hand, to lose ourselves in a mystical contemplation of God without considering His works will lead us to despise that which God meant for our good. He created all things to serve man who was created in His image and after His likeness; and in and with all things man is called to serve God in the beauty of holiness. God and His works, therefore, are not to be separated.

What we are to see in these works are various attributes or perfections of God which are displayed therein. Six of these attributes we find mentioned in our Catechism. Let us notice them very briefly. The first is God's power. This refers to that perfection distinguished in God's being whereby He is able to perform whatsoever He wills to do. This power is conceded to be both infinite and absolute. "With God all things are possible." Wisdom, the second attribute referred to by our Catechism, is that perfection in the Almighty whereby He uses His knowledge to reach the highest aims or purposes of His holy will by the very best means and methods. In the countless experiences of His children here upon earth this becomes one of the most blessed sources of strength to carry on. In the presence of God's wisdom we are conscious of our own ignorance. We cannot always understand or comprehend His ways, but we gradually learn to trust that because of His infinite wisdom His ways are the best for us. All things work for good to them that love Him. A third matter brought to our attention is the goodness of God. This is a very comprehensive term and what is designated by it manifests itself in various forms. When we think, for instance, of God's goodness toward His rational creatures, we speak of it as His love. And surely none of us will ever succeed in grasping the full meaning and content of God's love. When we think of God's goodness toward guilty, undeserving sinners, we speak of it as God's grace. It is this grace of God, imparted to His people, which not only saves them but inspires them to live worthily of their calling. When the goodness of God concerns itself with the miserable, we refer to it as God's mercy. His mercy is most tender and offers a wonderful solace to all who observe it in His dealings with His people.

Justice and truth are the other two virtues mentioned here by our Catechism. Justice is that perfection which assures us that God is righteous in all His doings. With our darkened understandings we sometimes are unable to see the justice of all of God's dealings with us. But if we by grace view the Lord's justice in the light of His infinite love, we are willing to confess that our God is perfect and holy in His righteousness. The divine attribute of truth tells us that God is consistent in all that He does. We express our opinion of man's consistency in the proverb: "Consistency, thou art a jewel." But our God is in truth and verity what He represents Himself to be. Consequently, on this attribute rests God's great faithfulness. We can trust Him because He is faithful and true. His Word is sure; His promises are kept and fulfilled. They that trust in Him shall never be put to shame.

Now, when we pray, "Hallowed be thy name," we are asking that we may sanctify, glorify and praise God in all His works in which all these various attributes or perfections of His are clearly displayed.

Knowing God in all His works we ask Him also to grant to us what we need to order and direct our whole life—our thoughts, words and actions—in such a way that His name may never be blasphemed, but rather honored and praised on our account. After what we have said in the first part of this sermon it will not be necessary to enlarge upon this matter here. We should never forget what Jesus said to His disciples: "Ye are the salt of the earth: but if the salt have lost his savour, wherewith shall it be salted? It is thenceforth good for nothing, but to be cast out, and to be trodden under foot of men. Ye are the light of the world. A city that is set on an hill cannot be hid." In the light of this word the Christian's attitude toward his neighbors should never be that of Cain, expressed in his question: "Am I my brother's keeper?" We as Christians have a responsibility toward all with whom we come in contact upon the highway of life. We should be sure that if they follow our example they will not walk in darkness but in the light. We need to be much concerned about this calling in these days of ours. It is so easy to forget it and hard to be mindful of it. This leads us to consider finally—

IV. THE PURPOSE OF THIS BASIC PETITION IN THE LORD'S PRAYER

By way of application we desire to notice this briefly. The first purpose is to lead us to God that we may glorify Him. We learn by experience that in Him is our strength. As often as we have leaned upon ourselves or upon other men we have been put to shame. In the test our and their weakness has been disappointing. All is *of Him,* in whom we believe and whom we would serve. In Him is our strength and our ability. But we also learn by experience that all things are *by Him;* and this teaches us to live a life of prayer. From day to day He must provide us with all we need. Even as we pray for our daily bread so we must pray that daily He may grant us to praise and glorify His Holy Name. And, finally, we learn by experience that all things are *unto Him.* We possess nothing that we can honestly call our own. All that we have received, we have received of Him. And though given to us, it still remains His. He has entrusted it to us as stewards that we may use all to His glory. Stewards of the household of God! What confidence our God has in us, that, though He knows us, He will make us His stewards. How grateful we ought to be and how sincere in our striving to be good stewards, that need not be ashamed in the day of the Lord.

The second purpose of this petition is to assure us that we have a place among God's children. A passion for the glorification of God is one of the marks of a child of God. Of course, we realize that any one can utter these words, "Hallowed be thy name"; but

that does not make it a petition. We read that no
one can say that Jesus is the Lord except by the Holy
Spirit. No one can say, "Abba, Father," but they who
are the children of God. The mind must be illumined
by the Spirit of light; the heart must be renewed by
the Spirit of life; the will must be brought into
subjection to the will of God by the Spirit of omnipotence, before we can really grasp and feel the meaning of this petition and sincerely take it upon our lips
as a prayer to God.

But as often as we do, we find ourselves one with
all the children of God. We love to think of the
angelic hosts as the great celestial chorus which sings
over and over again, to the praise of the Most High,
"Holy, Holy, Holy, is the Lord God Almighty; the
whole earth is full of His glory!" That chorus is one.
There are no discordant voices. The same applies to
God's children here upon earth. They are a mighty
company, gathered out of every people, kindred and
tongue. And how they differ in outward appearance!
Their race, color, nationality, dress, mode and customs
of living — these all are barriers that separate them
socially. But as often as the believers, individually or
jointly, lift up their voice in this prayer they are one
in Christ with all the children of God throughout the
whole earth. In this prayer all the barriers that separate
them disappear. Surely you must have noticed that it
is an inclusive prayer. Jesus did not teach us to say,
"My Father"; but He taught us all to say, "Our Father."
Oh, that we all may belong to that great multitude
who are united in the desire that God's name may be
glorified and recognize in that desire a proof of their
sonship!

The third purpose of this petition is to prepare us

for our own life's purpose. No doubt we have frequently asked ourselves what may be the purpose of our presence in this world. What are we here for anyway?

Unless we have learned to see our life in the light of divine revelation, it must seem useless to us. But when once we have seen it in that light we are willing to acknowledge that our fathers were right when they taught us that the supreme purpose of all things is the glory of God. That should be our aim in life. With all we are and with all we have we should seek to glorify our God. At his creation man was able to answer to that purpose. But having been separated from His God through wilful disobedience he is no longer willing or able in himself to answer to that purpose. The basic petition of the Lord's Prayer, "Hallowed be thy name," reminds us that this is the supreme object of our life and helps to fit us for this task. If we really pray this petition, it is our heart's desire that God shall receive of us the glory that is due to His name. How tremendously important, therefore, this basic petition of the Lord's Prayer is seen to be! We trust that we all may learn to see it in the right light and learn to pray it acceptably through the work of the Holy Spirit in our hearts and in our lives. If we pray it, though haltingly and with hesitation, because we fear that we have no right to pray it, we can be assured of our fellowship with Christ and with all who are His. If we refuse to pray it, or if we utter it without thought or consideration, the truth is not in us and we still stand in need of Him who alone can save from death and hell. He still invites all who are burdened with sin and heavy laden with guilt to come to him, that He may give them rest. If we have come and have experienced something of that rest, let us seek to serve Him aright. If we have not yet come, let us not harden our hearts, but call upon Him while He is ready to hear us, and draw nigh to Him while He is near.

XLVIII

Forty-Eighth Lord's Day

THY KINGDOM COME

Rev. William H. Rutgers, Th.D.

Scripture Reading: Matt. 3:24-50   *Text:* Matt. 6:10

THE BURDEN of this forty-eighth Lord's Day is a consideration of the second petition of the Lord's prayer: "Thy kingdom come." If we are to gain a proper understanding of this petition we must at the very outset remember that this is a *prayer* and that it is *one* of the petitions which our Lord taught His *disciples* to pray. Obviously there is the closest connection between the several petitions, and the interpretation given by our Instructor clearly demonstrates that only a Christian can pray this prayer. It was upon the specific request of His disciples, "Lord, teach us to pray," that Jesus taught them this prayer, which without fear of contradiction may safely be styled the Model Prayer.

A moment's reflection will serve to indicate why men have regarded it as a perfect pattern. It is a Christ-taught prayer. That in itself is most significant. Beyond that, several particulars might be mentioned which mark its excellence: its brevity, comprehensiveness, simplicity; its proper distribution of emphasis as to spiritual and material needs; and its arrangement of particulars, so that first things are first in order.

An examination of our personal prayers will show how far most of them are removed from this perfect model; how little concern there is in them for God's name, His kingdom and His will, and by way of contrast how large our own temporal needs loom up. Excellent indeed is the recommendation to pray the Lord's Prayer at least once each day, in order that our prayers may have proper poise and balance.

In our analysis of the separate petitions we ought to guard zealously against the danger, which is not at all fanciful, of disconnecting each petition from the *one prayer.* So profound are the implications and so rich is the content of each separate petition that one can very readily lose sight of the fact that the prayer is one perfect whole. Forgetting that the prayer is of one piece, and the whole is never greater than the sum of its parts, the result would be that we would have a number of unconnected parts. Apparently such a procedure would seriously impair the unity and the spirit of the prayer and would render a balanced understanding of it impossible.

Having been cautioned in our analysis of the prayer not to disconnect the various parts, it is equally important to remember that each petition has its own peculiar burden. Brief is this prayer, yet comprehensive, so that in a few words it covers the whole range of the *what* and the *manner* of our prayers. Each word in it counts; there is no vain repetition. Consequently we are invited to address ourselves, carefully and specifically, to a consideration of this second petition: "Thy kingdom come."

Our Instructor merely asks, "What is the second petition?" Strictly speaking, the answer might end with these words, "Thy kingdom come," for that is the sum and substance of the second petition. But since the authors of the Heidelberg Catechism aim to give instruction to Christians, they appended an interpretation to this petition, which we find in the answer to Question 123. This they conceived to be the content of what the Christian prays for when he utters the words: "Thy kingdom come."

Due to the nebulous and hazy notions that the average Christian of this present age holds as to the kingdom of God, it will be necessary to clarify the conception "kingdom of God," if we are intelligently to pray this petition. In spite of the colossal conceit and presumption of this age, it is characterized by a lack of careful and accurate information on almost any subject, especially when it concerns the concepts of the supernatural religion of Christianity. At best the average Christian has some flighty and sentimental knowledge of the religion he embraces. A little honest examination will prove that the information he has lacks definiteness and precision. Added to this, a faulty conception of the kingdom of God has loomed up large in Christian literature of the last quarter century—a conception that has been vigorously propagated and excessively pressed and popularized by the many Bible schools in our land—a conception that has been given a tremendous impetus by the notes appended to the Scofield Bible—and yet a conception which we as sons and daughters of the Reformation, as inheritors of the best that Protestantism has produced and which it has deposited in its creeds, cannot share.

Pressed therefore on the one hand by religious superficiality and on the other by a very popular, yet erroneous view of the kingdom of God, it is the more urgent that we make a careful survey as to what we mean by the phrase "the kingdom of God." Without such a clear conception of it we cannot intelligently pray this second petition nor can we understand the interpretation given of it by the authors of our Instructor.

The natural theme of our discussion is the kingdom of God. We propose to divide the material for our consideration in two parts. In the first we shall endeavor to set forth the Biblical and Reformed conception of the kingdom of God; in the second we shall devote ourselves to an elucidation of the answer given by the Instructor.

The kingdom of God! What a truly marvelous and tremendous conception it is! How grave the danger that we through our familiarity with the phrase lose the sense of its comprehensiveness, its profound meaning and its sublime beauty! Not incorrectly is it declared to be the one comprehensive term of the whole of the Master's teaching. Indeed it is a revelation, something like a fresh discovery that charms and fascinates, to turn to the Synoptic gospels of Matthew, Mark and Luke, and discover how frequently this subject—it is also called the kingdom of my Father, the kingdom of Heaven, the kingdom of Christ, the kingdom of the Son of Man — was on the lips of Jesus. The forerunner, John the Baptist, went forth crying, "Repent ye, for the kingdom of God is at hand." Jesus centered His teaching, given in the unforgettable parables and in exquisite, concrete symbolisms, about the kingdom—a kingdom that had ever existed since the dawn of history; a kingdom that by His incarnation and finished, vicarious work on the cross was a present fact; a kingdom, moreover, that is a progressive reality, which shall be

consummated at the Second Advent of our Lord. Just
for the reason that His coming again will mark the
perfect realization of His kingdom in the state of
glory, that coming is the one grand hope and fervent
longing of every Christian.

St. John in his Apocalypse wrestles with language
in the attempt to envisage some of the beauty, the
grandeur, the supreme joy and everlasting happiness
of those who shall enter the kingdom of glory. The
central theme of Jesus' teaching was the kingdom. He
exhorts men to seek entrance to that kingdom whatever the cost or sacrifice may be. He warns against
the pitfalls and obstacles which hinder or oppose our
entrance. He declares that some are not far from
the kingdom. He braces the courage of one who is
very near to it. He gives to the office-bearers of His
church the keys of the kingdom, with power to bind
or loose. In two of His superb beatitudes He describes
such as shall inherit the kingdom, namely, the poor
in spirit and those persecuted for righteousness' sake.
And He declares that the day will come when the believers of every nation and generation shall sit down
with Abraham in the kingdom of heaven. Whatever
else is true, the kingdom idea certainly was most prominent in the mind of Jesus.

The very conception of a kingdom implies a king
who has the rightful and recognized authority to rule.
God is both the rightful Ruler and the Absolute Sovereign over all things by virtue of being the Creator of
this universe. We usually distinguish between a divine
kingdom in which there is the exercise of sheer power
and one in which there is the exercise of grace, the
latter of which shall consummate in glory. The Bible
is full of the thought that God is the absolute sover·

eign Ruler over all things that exist. "The earth is the Lord's and the fulness thereof; the world and they that dwell therein. The Lord reigneth, he is clothed with majesty; the Lord is clothed with strength; for the Lord is a great God, and a great King above all Gods," declares the Psalmist. That sovereignty is exercised over all animate and inanimate creation—over plant and beast; over man and the angelic hosts of heaven. We have but to recall the prophetic word of Daniel, who, speaking of this God, says: "He doeth according to his will in the army of heaven and among the inhabitants of the earth."

In this kingdom, wherein there is the exercise of sheer power, we do not speak of a conscious, willing obedience to God's laws or transgressions of those laws. Rather, in this kingdom of power we can properly speak only of a compulsory obedience, one that has no moral value. And yet, even so, it is a most comforting truth for the Christian to embrace, especially in times of trouble, amid tumult and confusion, in periods of national disaster and peril and in seasons when the transientness of all things temporal is impressed upon him, calmly to retreat into the inner chamber and there confidently to lift up his eyes to the heavens and say: "The Lord reigneth." Such firm assurance stabilizes; such unwavering confidence steadies. It affords poise and balance. It guards against panicky fear and safely leads us through the morasses of despair and the sloughs of despondency.

Nevertheless, not the kingdom of power but that of grace is the burden of the prayer, "Thy kingdom come." In this kingdom, God, and very especially Christ, our Mediator, is the King. The essence of the law that is exercised in this kingdom of grace is love; the rational

and moral subjects who are the citizens of this kingdom must render willing obedience to the law of that
kingdom. Consequently, not God's sovereignty but
rather God's faithfulness and man's responsibility as
an image-bearer of God; not a compulsion by force
but love as manifested in grace to depraved and fallen
creatures, are the predominant notes in this kingdom
of which our text speaks. The kingdom of God in this
sense may then be defined as the rule or will of God
established in the hearts of regenerated men, which
rule or will is and progressively increases to be the
operative principle that motivates the Christian's life,
gives direction to and determines the purpose of living.
Citizens of this kingdom live God-centered lives, as
opposed to a life that is self-centered. In the last analysis this is the one all-important concern of life: to
be assured that we are members of that kingdom, in
distinction from the kingdoms of this world. These
latter may be multiple in manifestation, duration and
design, yet in actual fact, members of these kingdoms
are actuated by principles woven on one loom, having
the selfsame texture; and that is the natural self.

One needs but to read the infallible record of what
is in natural man, as Paul penned it in his Epistle to
the Romans, and one may verify its trustworthiness by
observation and a critical examination of history, to
be convinced that there is nothing to boast of, and that
kingdoms comprised of such citizens cannot but end
in dismal defeat, in that which cheats and blasts man's
fairest dreams and fondest hopes. To be within or
without the kingdom of God is the one line of cleavage,
the one antithesis that separates men and men; we are
either those in whose hearts God is enthroned so that
we are prompted by Divine love and equipped by

sovereign grace to willingly subject ourselves to His law; or we are those who keep self, or others like self, enthroned, and live in accordance with laws man has made.

Fundamentally we meet at this point *the* difference between Christianity and everything that is not Christian; of theism as opposed to humanism of every brand; of supernaturalism versus naturalism; of revealed religion over against man-made makeshifts; of divine certainty contrasted to human speculation. Citizens of the kingdom of God recognize Christ as their King and Lord. By a faithful use of the means of grace and gracious operation of the Holy Spirit in our lives we are brought into a more complete subjection to His will. He becomes the supreme object of our love and adoration. In Him all trust is reposed for protection against that which would defeat the rule of His law within us. To Him we look for ever-present help, and through Him we confidently expect one day to receive the crown of victory.

A faithful consideration of each of these particulars will convince us that such a kingdom ideal actually controls and governs the Christian's life. The one consuming passion of every Christ-follower ought to be to promote the King's rule: first of all that His law, which conditions human happiness, might be more regnant in us, manifesting itself in Christ-like living; and secondly, that through such a life of confession and practice the King's rule may be more firmly established and extended in the lives of others.

The kingdom of God, in this strict sense of God's will governing and being the actuating principle of human life, existed in Paradise, before Adam sinned. But man by his wilful transgression and open rebellion disturbed the harmony between God's will and man's. After this defection the kingdom of God could exist in its true state only in heaven. About the throne of God in heaven are the myriads of obedient angels that are ever ready to accomplish His will. There is a kingdom of heaven in this true sense that the King is recognized and His rightful rule accomplished by willing and loving obedience among these angelic hosts. The kingdom of heaven is thus clearly distinguished from the locality, heaven, on the one hand; and from the state of the saved, salvation, on the other. God graciously intervened and revealed His plan of a covenant of grace, which was realized by the redemptive work of Jesus our Mediator; and so this King's rule is once again established on earth in the hearts of men, namely, the regenerate.

The first foregleam of this gracious promise is recorded in Genesis 3:15, after which it was progressively unfolded in type and symbol and prophetic utterance during the whole of the Old Testament dispensation. The Old Testament revelation culminated in kingdom prophecy and in the Messiah who would be the King of that Messianic kingdom. It is very apparent in these kingdom prophecies that the kingdom is both a present reality and that which must be consummated, fully realized, in the future. On the one hand the kingdom is presented as already existing and on the other it is presented as coming. The Davidic kingship or kingdom is an adumbration, a shadow, of that which will one day be perfect reality. So predominant is both the Messiah, the king idea, and the Messianic kingdom concept in the Old Testament revelation, that we may fairly well group all of its teaching under these two heads: first, teaching that concerns the coming King;

and second, that which gives information as to the kingdom.

The prophecies of Isaiah and of Micah give us some of the clearest descriptions of the coming king. He shall be of humble birth; shall be born of a Virgin; He shall come forth as a rod out of the stem of Jesse, and a Branch; from Bethlehem shall come forth One who is to be ruler in Israel. Though of humble birth He shall be the true King, a Ruler upon whom the Spirit of God rests, the Spirit of wisdom and understanding, of counsel and might; He shall rule in equity, righteousness shall be enthroned, and His people He shall protect and save from all enemies. While the blessings of that kingdom will consist mainly of spiritual realities, it cannot be denied that there are also some material blessings that shall accompany the spiritual. Such a kingdom of righteousness, of peace and of prosperity, will He establish on earth and, much to the chagrin of nationalistic-minded Judaism, this kingdom will be universal; it will demonstrate itself to be the realization of the promise given to Abraham: "In thy seed shall all nations be blessed."

The fatal blemish of Judaism was that it put excessive emphasis on the material blessings, the "this worldly" characteristics of that kingdom, and the erroneous conception it cherished regarding the purpose and mission of the coming Messiah. Only then do we understand the teaching of John the Baptist and of Jesus when we have taken cognizance of the perverted ideas of the coming King and the kingdom as held by Judaism. Jesus' teaching is in perfect consonance with the spirit and reality of the Old Testament revelation. Judaism had externalized what was intended to be internal. It emphasized the material at the expense of the spiritual. What was intended to be universal it narrowed down to the local. The heavenly it dragged down to the earthly. The portrayal of the heavenly kingdom with its heavenly Jerusalem as the capital and seat of the true kingdom of God, is understood as a description of the earthly Jerusalem. It conceived of the kingdom solely as a present fact and neglected to think of it as a blessed hope. Once more, Judaism differed sharply from the teaching of Jesus in its conception of how this kingdom would be ushered in, by what method it would be effectively realized.

Just this sharp difference brought Jesus into frequent collision with the Pharisees and the nationalistic-minded Jews of His day. Judaism believed that by some manifestation of God's Almighty power this kingdom would suddenly be ushered in, all enemies would at the twinkling of an eye be vanquished, the earthly kingdom would be set up, and the Jews would reign with Him forever and ever. Jesus presented the kingdom as one that cometh not with observation, but rather as a leaven, whose power and influence would permeate the whole lump. A certain writer has quite accurately expressed the difference between Judaism and Jesus by asserting that Judaism emphasized the first half of the phrase "the kingdom of God," whereas Jesus stressed both. The Jews stopped short with an emphasis on "the kingdom"; Jesus made the last two words, "of God," just as important.

When considering the method by which this kingdom is to be realized, in which particular Jesus differed so sharply with Judaism, we may conveniently point out the difference between Biblical Christianity and that which proudly claims to be the twentieth-century interpretation of it: the so-called "social gospel." This is the gospel of all Liberalism and Modernism, and while it claims to embody all essential truths of the old gospel, differing from it only in this that it has fitted the old truths to the twentieth-century patterns of thought, we may be positively assured that it is a gospel of naturalism and humanism, the exact antithesis of the old gospel of supernaturalism, or Biblical Christianity.

As to the method of realizing the kingdom, the social gospel of Modernism and Liberalism expects this to be accomplished by reformation, by schemes, laws, more efficient educational policies, better environment and improved sanitary conditions. It tacitly assumes the inherent goodness of man. Sin, in this social gospel, is ignorance, lack of proper control of our urges and drives, a backward pull of an outgrown good, a remnant of animal instinct, a vestige of the tiger and the ape characteristics, which training, education and civilization will eventually eradicate.

It needs no argument to convince anyone that such conceptions would subvert the whole of the supernatural religion of the cross; would signify the deathblow to the beliefs of our fathers and would lead to the impoverishment of our faith. A pious Christian might then still hold to such phrases as "sovereign, irresistible grace"; "Jesus Christ as a vicarious sin-bearer and a propitiation for our sins"; and "redemption solely through the shed blood of Jesus our Mediator." Sentimentally and emotionally such a pious Christian might derive some comfort from such language; yet in reality the Liberalist and Modernist who heralds a social gospel declares that these phrases are outgrown and outmoded patterns of thought and that they no longer serve us.

Their method of realizing the kingdom is one of social reformation; they approach humanity from the outside; the agency is machinery. The method that Jesus advocated and that Christianity advances is one of regeneration, of conversion, of individual consecration. The approach is from the inside; the agency is the efficacious operation of the Holy Spirit in the individual hearts of men, whereby the spiritual merits and benefits of the vicarious sin-bearer Jesus Christ are savingly applied to us and we, by a process of progressive sanctification, are fashioned after the perfect pattern, Jesus Christ. Thus the kingdom of God is both a present fact and at the same time we may speak of it as continually coming. As God's will increasingly becomes the actuating rule of our life, the influence of such a life will promote the extension of that kingdom in the hearts and lives of others and thus will widen its sphere of influence in this world.

The relation of the Church, as a visible organization instituted by our Lord, to the kingdom of God is most vital. An adequate discussion of this particular would require more space than can be allotted. The church that measures up to the divine requirements, namely, the pure preaching of the Word, the Scriptural administration of the sacraments and the faithful exercise of Christian discipline, is the most effective agency to promote the welfare and extension of the kingdom of God. While it is possible for one to be a member of the kingdom and yet not of any church, this is both abnormal and rare. Nor does it follow that every confessing member of the visible Church is by virtue of that fact a member of the kingdom of God. Whereas the Church is a temporal agency promoting and extending the kingdom, its design being realized at the Second Advent of our Lord, the kingdom is the abiding reality. The social aspect of the kingdom is most clearly demonstrated in the activity of the Church; and it is through this agency that the kingdom wields its mightiest influence, displays its unfading glory and manifests its divine dynamic and immortal life in the midst of this world. Without exaggeration or presumption it may be asserted that the Church gathers in the sheaves for the kingdom harvest.

Summing up the teaching of Jesus concerning this kingdom, we should make mention of the following particulars. It is a kingdom not of this world, but from above; a kingdom within the kingdoms of this world. Whereas all earthly kingdoms, after running their course, vanish from the face of the earth, the kingdom of God survives. It traffics in spiritual goods: forgiveness of sins, righteousness and eternal life. While mainly spiritual it also has a material counterpart, so that both body and soul will share its benefits and one day enter the consummated kingdom. Jesus represented the kingdom both as a present fact and as that which is coming, for which should be offered our fervent prayer, "Thy kingdom come." The conditions for entrance to that kingdom are regeneration, faith, conversion. This kingdom is universal; in it earthly distinctions have no validity. To belong to it is purely a matter of grace and is granted to those who trust in the merits secured for them by Jesus our Mediator. At His coming again this kingdom will enter into the state of glory. It is this kingdom for which we pray in the words: "Thy kingdom come."

Our Instructor gives us an interpretation of it which we Christians heartily endorse. It is paraphrased as follows in the answer to question 123 of the Heidelberg Catechism: "So rule us by thy Word and Spirit that we may submit ourselves more and more to Thee; pre-

serve and increase Thy Church; destroy the works of
the devil, every power that exalts itself against Thee,
and all wicked counsels conceived against Thy holy
Word until the perfection of Thy kingdom arrive wherein Thou shalt be all in all." A little reflection on
this answer will serve to demonstrate how precisely
our Instructor interprets the kingdom-idea as the Bible
reveals it, and that this answer is in consonance with the
definition, the characterization, particulars and method
of its realization as we have presented it. The three
clauses in the answer supply the divisions which pro-
portionally distribute the emphasis that is required.

The kingdom of God, we have asserted, is the rule
or will of God established in the hearts of the regenerated. This divine will is and progressively increases to be the operative principle that motivates the
Christian's life, gives direction to and determines the
purpose of living. As such, the Christian lives a God-
centered or Christ-centered life. His one supreme desire
is that he may decrease in order that Christ may increase. Is that not exactly what our Heidelberg Catechism intends to convey and impress upon us, when it
declares that to pray, "Thy kingdom come," signifies
first of all: "so rule us by Thy Word and Spirit that
we may submit ourselves more and more to Thee."
When God's or Christ's will becomes the ruling and
governing law of our life, His kingdom will be the
more firmly established. Obviously this stresses the
true conception of the Kingdom; namely, that it is both
a present fact and a growing, progressive reality.

We do well carefully to note the words *"rule* us"
in this first clause. That verb has a few implications
which so clearly point to the kingdom-idea. That there
is such a rule implies that there is a law which has

been promulgated as a rule of life, a king who as lawgiver exercises this rule and a realm in which there are subjects who obey this law and are ruled by this king. Self-rule is impossible; as citizens of the kingdom we willingly submit to the King's rule. Since that is true, it is plain that only a Christian can pray this prayer, for natural man is a lover of self, enthrones self and refuses undivided and loyal allegiance to the Almighty King of kings.

The agency whereby this rule of God or Christ is realized in us is His Word and Spirit. That consideration places upon us the solemn obligation to give diligent heed to the Word of God. If this is an earnest prayer it will incite us to a faithful study of the Word of God that we may ascertain what God's will requires of us. Appalling ignorance of the Word of life, the revealed will of God, is one of the sad indexes of this superficial and presumptuous age. Pious Christians are praying for a revival of the old-time religion. Many schemes are proposed and programs launched to hasten such a spiritual awakening. Judged by the infallible standards or method which God prescribed, most of these schemes and programs are experiments manufactured by the fancy of men. God's method of promoting and extending this kingdom is not by machinery, not by observation and glamorous display, nor by schemes that operate from the outside, but by individual consecration, devotion and loyalty to Christ; by individual regeneration and conversion; by God's revealed will governing the lives of men. Conditions will be ripe for a revival only when we make earnest effort to know that will of God, and sincerely pray for the illumination of the Spirit of God to illumine our eyes, to enlighten our minds and to translate that will of

God into throbbing, living principles that govern our life.

Lord, may Thy kingdom come. May it come in us; may Thy will more fully regulate our lives and govern us. Thy will conditions our happiness. Living in accordance with it makes life blessed, telling, influential; it imparts to us blessed comfort and peace. That Thy kingdom may come, lead us by Thy Spirit into Thy matchless truth; help us to live consistent lives; with manly fortitude to quit the ways of sin and to depart from the workers of iniquity. May we consciously consider our chief concern in life to be the promotion and extension of Thy kingdom. The lofty words of Paul: "For me to live is Christ," will mark the boundaries of such a life's program.

Thy kingdom come: that means also, according to our Instructor: "preserve and increase Thy Church." God has commanded and made arrangement that those in whom is the kingdom of God form the Church, the visible body of Christ in this dispensation. The Church is not the kingdom; it is rather the agency or instrument which most effectively promotes the welfare and extension of this kingdom of God. Through the agency of the Church the members of the kingdom collectively exert their influence in this world.

As a Divine institution, the Church instructs the citizens of the kingdom, clarifying the will of God and encouraging the members of the kingdom by declaring to them the present glorious privileges which are theirs and likewise impressing upon them the solemn duties to which these obligate them. The one God-ordained agency to dispense the gifts of the kingdom is the Church of Jesus Christ. As a rule the kingdom progresses only in the measure in which the Church of

Jesus Christ flourishes. So vital is the relation between the Church and the kingdom that by some the former is regarded as the visible manifestation of the kingdom—which is correct when we allow for the proper reservations.

As the body of Christ we would expect the law of our blessed Christ to be more clearly in evidence in this visible Church. Sadly we must confess that not infrequently the Church is torn by dissension and misunderstanding. May these dissensions and disputes never embitter us but rather make us hunger the more for the true bread of life and for a clearer comprehension of God's revealed will.

Therefore, when we pray for the coming of the kingdom, we must also consciously pray for the extension and preservation of the Church. Since we can accomplish our best work in the Church only when we are active members, this prayer obligates us to confess the name of Christ, to be confessing members in the Church. We must be willing to be used to further God's kingdom; more than that, there must be a firm determination on our part to do so. The Church is a means He has ordered to foster the kingdom. Shall we refuse to honor that Divine instrument? And yet, how many anemic, sickly church-members there are! How quick they are to criticize; how slow to encourage; how measured and calculated the sacrifices, if they can be styled such—for the Church. How lavish the spending on self! What thoughts of self burden our prayers; how meager our requests for the welfare and prosperity of the Church; for the ambassadors of the Cross—that the pure, unadulterated Word of God may be preached; that the sacraments be purely administered; and that the painful but utterly needful task of Christian discipline be rigorously and fearlessly executed!

Lord, may Thy kingdom come! To that end, preserve Thy Church; save it from the encroachments of Modernism and Liberalism, which will impoverish our faith. Preserve for us the rich heritage of our fathers given such rich expression in the historic creeds of Christendom. Preserve for us the faithful interpretation of Thy truth. Preserve us from the fads and fancies of men who attempt to improve upon the revealed mission of the Church, upon its purpose in this world, but who in the end would enfeeble its power and defeat its design. To the end that Thy Church may be preserved, may we dedicate and consecrate our talents to Thee; zealously guard her ramparts; uphold her fair name; deliver her from the dead, inert mass of nominal and hereditary Christians which retards her progress and cools her fervor. Preserve Thy Church, Lord, from enemies within and without; preserve her spiritual vitality; preserve her from conformity to the world. Impress upon her members that her program by which she will succeed is non-conformist, is protestant, and that she is begotten from above. Grant her the throb of immortal life and make her conscious of her all-conquering faith.

Not only do we pray for the preservation of the Church; we also include in the prayer, "Thy kingdom come," the petition that this Church may increase. It must increase inwardly and outwardly. Her power and influence in this world will increase in equal ratio to the deepening, the increase, of our understanding of God's truth and with the progressive application of it to the full round of the Christian's life. Consequently there must be on the part of the Christian who prays,

"Thy kingdom come," a profound desire to know God's truth.

Make an honest examination of yourself to determine whether or not this is an actual fact. Test the sincerity of your prayer as to this particular, by the material you read, and by the question whether you have seasons of meditation and quiet contemplation of God's infallible Word. Ask yourself the question: Do I respond to the opportunities offered which may, by God's grace, increase my grasp of the truth? Only as we increase here can the church of which we are a member increase. In every church there are such societies in which it is possible for each and all to make a personal contribution. Christianity is a self-propagating religion; the light which you have received you must share with others. If the Church is to increase, the gospel must be presented in all of its gripping challenge and fitted to the needs and thought-forms of the day in which we live.

If the Church increases inwardly the outward manifestation of this growth will be in evidence. This may be applied to the whole gamut of kingdom activity. Foremost stands the missionary endeavor. How many thousands there still are, even in this enlightened, Christian nation, who are wholly ignorant of the claims of Christ, who, in a word, are but civilized pagans! Think of the millions who still bow down to idols of wood and stone, to gods of their own fashioning; who mutilate their bodies, live in utter ignorance, and who die in abject misery. Be certain of this, if any church has lost her desire to answer the missionary challenge, and cancels in her program the great commission of Christ, it is retrograding, her life is ebbing away, and though she may have the name that she lives, yet in actual fact the living throb and dynamic of Christ's immortal life has departed from her. There are untold opportunities in every community to engage in some form of missionary endeavor, and by our gifts we may do so by proxy.

Besides missions, there are other activities which increase the Church outwardly and so promote and extend the kingdom. Members of the Church should use their influence to draw others within the fold. What a potent power the Christian schools are to promote the Church and the kingdom! May God see fit to bless these schools and may we as Christians think of them when we pray, "Thy kingdom come." The Church will increase by our diligence in the spread of Christian literature; in the erection and maintenance of institutions of mercy; in collective Christian action against all that which is organized to trample her to the dust of the earth. In spite of her inconsistencies and errors, the Church of Jesus Christ still is the world's greatest benefactor and the record of her history is most enviable. For her our fervent prayers are offered: "Lord, preserve and increase Thy Church."

"Thy kingdom come," that is, rule us by Thy Word and Spirit; preserve and increase Thy Church, that the kingdom may come in this world; and that we may take the offensive against all the machinations of the devil, who plans to frustrate God's purpose in this world. Our Instructor expresses this thought as follows: "destroy the works of the devil, every power that exalts itself against Thee and all wicked counsels conceived against Thy holy Word." This prompts us to think of the organized efforts of atheism which would put God out of this universe and banish Him from our thinking. In whichever way the kingdoms of the world may be divided, there is an underlying unity among them all; for they are one in their opposition to the one kingdom which God is establishing. There are but two forces battling for mastery in this world: the kingdom of darkness over against the kingdom of light; the kingdom of the lie directly opposed to that of the truth. The hosts of the one are led by Satan, by the spirit of the Antichrist; the others have as their leader Jesus the Lord. While the spirit of today is one of sympathetic appreciation, of the vain attempt to seek similarities, let us be done with such a philosophy of compromise, for in no particular are these kingdoms to be harmonized; their yoking is ever unequal. Eternal vigilance is the price we shall have to pay to retain and hold fast what we have.

What opposition this furtherance of the kingdom of God meets today in the spirit of our age! Besides open rebellion, as we meet it in atheism, we must contend against the more subtle humanistic, antichristian theories as popularized in the daily press, defended from many a Modernistic pulpit, and presented by means of radio and TV. Last but not least, the kingdom is opposed by the pagan ideals of the modern educational policies, the education given the nation's children and youth—an education that fears not God and recognizes not the Lordship of Christ. On every hand there is wholesale denial of the supernatural. Ours is an age of carnality, of flesh and brawn. The ideals men have are low and easily attainable. It is an age of crass materialism and naked naturalism. Examine the filth of our public press; the corruption and wickedness perpetrated by those seated in high places of authority; the stark realism of modern art; the sensational novel that appeals to the baser appetites of man. Surely the most casual

observation will convince us all that this is a day in
which the fervent prayer is demanded of all Christians,
"Thy kingdom come"; that is, destroy the works of
the devil, every power that exalts itself against Thee,
and all wicked counsels conceived against Thy Word.
How the scoffers and doubters of the Word have increased in this supercilious presumptuous age which
styles itself "scientific." A lack of confidence in the
old Bible would remove the very foundation on which
the Church rests. Praise God, the old Book will stand;
truth cannot be defeated. Storms of doubt and criticism
may rage, the angry billows may beat against this Rock,
yet it stands secure, able to weather any storm.

For nearly two thousand years this kingdom gospel
has been proclaimed, and yet it is so far from being
realized. The kingdom demands peace. Yet are there
wars and rumors of wars. "Cyclones of passion are
devastating the world." In every nation we hear the
rumblings of revolution, of socialism and anarchism.
There is dissatisfaction on every hand. Unrest, turmoil
and confusion characterize the nations, so that the
hearts of the faithful nearly fail for fear. The kingdom demands love. Instead we find hatred, jealousy,
avarice. Far too many of us take a passive attitude, as
if our witness and protest against it will be of no
avail since conditions are incurably evil and past cor-
rection. But with that attitude we forget the very purpose for which God made us citizens of the kingdom.
Ye are the salt of the earth, the light of the world!
Remember it! The kingdom demands righteousness; but
the one policy that has motivated most nations is that
might makes right. God's kingdom demands purity,
but where are the pure hearts and the clean hands?
How much there is today that is calculated to soil our

hands, pollute our hearts and contaminate our imaginations!

Our earnest and fervent prayer is, "Father, Thy kingdom come." May it come in us that we may give undivided allegiance to our Lord, and may we submit ourselves unreservedly to His will. Wilt Thou, O Lord, preserve and increase Thy Church. Destroy the works of the devil, to the end that the day may be hastened when the full perfection of Thy kingdom arrives and Thou shalt be all in all. While our hearts are saddened when we observe how far this kingdom of God is from its perfect realization, this is the one great encouragement for every Christian: a day is coming when the kingdom will be ushered into its state of glory. That glorious consummation will occur at the coming of our Saviour. The glorious promise of His coming again beckons us to a blessed hope and bids us to labor on, faithful to His Word and strong in His might. Through the darkness and gloom of despair appear the flashes of eternal light; amid the discordant notes of confusion and tumult sounds the harmonious note of peace. Wistfully do we gaze to the heavens, and with keen anticipation do we expect His coming. Our prayer is, "Thy kingdom come; Lord Jesus, come, yea, come quickly." And as we listen for His answer, we hear Him say: "Lo, I come quickly."

XLIX

Forty-Ninth Lord's Day

THY WILL BE DONE

Rev. Henry Evenhouse

Scripture Reading: John 4:34

PRECISION OF MEANING in the use of religious and theological terms is almost a lost art today. A strange reversal has taken place. In the period of the early Christian church, in the middle ages, and certainly in the time of the Reformation, accuracy of expression was sought after, so that in the sphere of religion there was the growth of terminology. At the same time, in the spheres of the natural sciences, in the measure that such were known, there was a great deal of ambiguity and ignorance. Today, with the amazing advances in industrial science and in natural sciences, there has been an emphasis on precision machinery, accuracy of definition, and with it, a precision of insight. In the natural sciences it is not suitable to be more or less correct. Yet in religion, people today often are content with cloudiness. We face in religion the tragic loss of careful definition; and the insistence upon it arouses with many impatience and nausea. We should however cherish the possession of careful definition; and it is the justifiable pride of the Reformed faith that it does come out and define its position.

There is considerable usage of the name God. The reluctance of men to define what they mean by this name is familiar. The name has become for many a general all-inclusive term to cover up the mystery of the great beyond. Frequently Christian people simply take for granted that the God of their friends, whosoever or whatever that may be, is necessarily the God of whom they have learned in the Christian home and church. When we insist on restricting the usage of this term to the Father Almighty, Maker of heaven and earth, who is the God of Abraham, Isaac and Jacob, and is the Father of our Lord Jesus Christ, we are said to be intolerant and bigoted. It is also so when we speak of the matter of prayer. We increasingly find nominal Christians classifying all prayers together, suggesting sincerity to be the real test. The intelligent Christian, however, has the term definitely prescribed in line with the Biblical instructions. Prayer is true and valid prayer in the Christian sense of the word when it is offered in true faith and in the name of the only High Priest, our Lord. When Jesus uttered the Lord's Prayer we may be sure of it that it had very definite content. In this sermon I am interested in calling your attention to some matters that are certainly implied in this petition: "Thy will be done on earth as it is in heaven." I would say that it expresses a positive faith. It expresses a living ideal. It also expresses a hearty commitment. A person cannot rightly use this prayer lacking either of these three elements. That does not mean that each must fully present to our consciousness when we utter these words, but they must in principle be present in mind and heart. Just as when we conclude our prayer, we know that it must be in the name of Jesus. We need not always expressly mention this, but, as a principle and a spirit it is always necessary. So when we say "Thy will be done on earth as it is in heaven," we must have a positive faith, a living ideal and a hearty consecration.

A POSITIVE FAITH

By positive faith I mean faith with a very specific content. It is evident that the suppliant needs faith in God. That is assumed as we are dealing with one who is praying to God. Here the specific content of faith refers to the will of God. "Thy will be done" means that the suppliant believes that God has a will, that that will is knowable, that it is good, and that it is important for us today.

There is a will of God. We speak of the will of God which is secret and that which is revealed. The former is the decree of God of which man knows nothing save as it unfolds itself in the acts of God. God has a working will which we cannot know, and from before the foundations of the earth He has established His purposes. It is not this will of God that is referred to in the Lord's Prayer. The hidden will of God will be done, the sin of man or the gates of hell notwithstanding. In the Lord's Prayer the will of God referred to is His revealed will which we have received from Him in the Bible.

We must consider the question of God's will being an actuality. The Scripture leaves us in no doubt, but the world which ignores the Scripture prefers to speak of the laws of nature and the popularly accepted laws of morality as all being part of the very nature of the universe, and quite such as they are apart from God. The Christian knows better. Already in the Garden of Paradise God's will definitely was given, and the duty of obedience was given to man. In the Old Testament we have abundance of testimony to God's will and it is usually referred to as "the Law."

The will of God is not a matter of natural law. It is expressive of God's mind and character, and is given to us from above. Let me indicate from two different sources how men speak of law and right. The notorious Karl Marx suggests that "law, morality, and religion . . . are bourgeois prejudices behind which lurk in ambush bourgeois interests." That is the communist conception of law; but, if we turn to the man often considered the dean of American education, John Dewey, we find that he says essentially the same thing. In his book, "Human Nature and Conduct" we read, "We are forced therefore to consider the nature and origin of that control of human nature with which morals has been occupied. And the fact which is forced upon us when we raise this question is the existence of classes. Control has been invested in oligarchy." The upshot of the matter for either of these men is that the laws which society recognizes as moral laws are essentially the creation of a ruling group, who thereby sought to secure their position over the subjects. Radical and revolutionistic as this may be, we have that conception in many quarters of our present day life. The Christian however looks upon law as originally from above: God spoke from Sinai, and Christ gave clarification, but no nullification, in the New Testament. The will of the Lord is revealed and we may know it.

The will of the Lord is good. The book of Psalms is rich with appreciative testimony of God's law. The closing verses of Psalm 19 are complete in declaring the excellence of God's law and will. "The law of the Lord is perfect, converting the soul; the testimony of the Lord is sure, making wise the simple; the statutes of the Lord are right, rejoicing the heart; the commandment of the Lord is pure, enlightening the eyes; the fear of the Lord is clean, enduring forever; the judgments of the Lord are true and righteous altogether. More to be desired are they than gold, yea, than much fine gold." We have in this psalm the glory of God as evident in nature, and then the writer proceeds to tell how the revealed law of God displays His glory in the moral universe.

We are not just content with a quotation to assure ourselves that there is the good will of God. This will is good because it is from God. It is good in that it reflects God. The heavens reflect the power and majesty of the Creator. The mystery of salvation causes Paul to cry out, "O the depth of the riches both of the wisdom and knowledge of God!" Concerning the law of God we hear the Psalmist say, "It is my meditation all the day." This certainly does not mean that he sits and ponders the several laws as just so many legal enactments. Of course not. When he meditates on the law of God he is seeing in that law the mirror of the creator of the law. That law is an expression of God's moral excellence, of His holiness and beauty. When we speak of the law of God we have not a group of arbitrary divine decisions before us. We are dealing with eternal principles of righteousness. Dr. Macartney in his book, *Christian Faith and the Spirit of the Age,* says, "The English philosopher, John Locke, had it in mind to write a work on ethics, but he finally abandoned the project, saying that in the New Testament we have a perfect system of ethics, one upon which it is impossible to make any improvement. The Gospel contains so perfect a body of ethics, that reason may be excused for that inquiry, since she may find man's duty clearer and easier in revelation than in herself."

In considering the faith expressed in this petition we confess that there is a will of God, that it is knowable, that it is good and that it is abidingly important. Let me briefly indicate that God's law which is given to men as a moral code is never alterable and ever an obligation, and important today. Obedience was the duty in Paradise and that requirement has never been changed. Ceremonial laws may and do vary but the laws of morality as taught in the Bible, as the expressions of God's own character, change no more than does the Lord Himself. We do have many in our day, both within and without the church, who speak of changing laws. Unfortunately, the church has always had to contend with the antinomians, Christians who do violence to Scripture teachings of right and wrong. There is a more pressing factor in our present day which we would do well to note. The opinion prevails that we can stem the tide of immorality and vice and crime with the creation of human laws, and that there is enough stamina in the human command to restrain the beast of sin. Shall we seek to stem the avalanche of unrighteousness with the voice of man? Must we have mudbanks to hold back wickedness or shall we have "the stern masonry of God's law"?

It is because God has spoken that we must obey. It is because God has spoken that we truly know what is right and what is wrong. The will of the Lord is known, and His will is our marching order. If the morality cultivated in America is of no higher order than that cultivated by the Nazi, which is admittedly human, there is no reason to assume ours to be better.

The will of God is not to be challenged. For the Christian it is the light on his path of duty.

A LIVING IDEA

When Jesus said "as it is done in heaven," He was speaking of an actual realm in which God's law was revealed, and in which there was perfect obedience. The perfect obedience was such as Christ Himself did render during the days of His flesh. The obedience was such as Adam was called upon to render in the garden of Paradise; and it is such obedience as will one day be realized in the glorified church.

Jesus knew of heaven from immediate experience, and as the Son of God, He, though on earth, had joyous recollections of the angels' obedience to their God. The obedience of angels is a matter of considerable interest. We know that the devil and his followers were ejected from heaven because of their failure to recognize rightly the true Lordship in heaven. The true angels however, render a flawless and immediate obedience to God.

The duties of angels as portrayed in the Bible vary as to attractiveness. Their tasks are sometimes delightsome for performance, as when the angel Gabriel was sent with the greeting—"Hail thou that art highly favored, the Lord is with thee." Other duties are infinitely somber as when the angel of the Lord stands in the path of Balaam brandishing the sword of death, or when, as in II Sam. 24:16, "The angel stretched out his hand upon Jerusalem to destroy it." But it is noteworthy that whatever their task may be, it is done in ready and with unqualified obedience. Their loyalty to the will of their Lord is absolute. A contrary will or preference does not enter in. They recognize that the will of the Lord as given to them is good and right and they have but to do His bidding.

Just recently an interesting book was published on the Lord's Prayer by the prominent airplane designer, Igor Sikorsky. This book has fascination since it comes from one whose attentions we might have considered wholly given to matters of earth. He speaks too of this petition. He speaks of the marvel of the predictability of an eclipse "with a precision of minutes and miles thousands of years ahead. This suggests wonderful order just as the efficiency of the sun and stars suggests wisdom and intelligence in their design. The secret of the precision of the universe lies in the gravitational force which makes itself known everywhere in all the universe. This gravitational force results in a team work, a free and voluntary co-operation of countless trillions of trillions of particles, each of them free, yet altogether maintaining the miraculous precision of the operation of the heavenly mechanism that permit prediction of an astronomic event within a few seconds thousands of years ahead."

From this study of the operation of the heavenly machines he draws an analogy, and says—"We can imagine multitudes of intelligent and powerful beings of an order higher than our own dwelling and acting in this heaven-universe completely free, yet in absolute harmony, reunited among themselves and united each and all of them with the Lord of the universe by an overwhelming feeling of good will. It is into this company that Christ invited us and opened the door by His words, acts and sacrifice" (p. 33).

Sikorsky suggests that should some particle get out of the gravitational force of the universe it would literally end in outer darkness. Within the framework of

God's universe, he finds that all matter, all particles, ally themselves together to bring about this perfect precision which the astronomer can discover. The awe-inspiring majesty of heavenly precision speaks of the high order of existence where God's law is observed; in this instance, His laws of the planetary bodies. The fact remains, however, that in all the precision of the heavenly body we cannot observe a moral factor or a personal choice of any kind. The order referred to by Christ is the higher order of the angelic hosts who are moral creatures and have the powers of spirit. The order of the universe is non-moral and non-intelligent. It is of the order of nature. When Christ says "As in heaven" He is not thinking of a mere natural order. He speaks of an exalted order in which the obedience to law is not of the nature of gravity but in which the moral and spiritual qualities of men enter. The angels in their order offer an ideal pattern which men are to emulate. The Kingdom of God is a Kingdom of spiritual beings in which freedom reigns but in which the freedom expresses itself in gladsome faithfulness to God's will. The angels render that obedience out of worshipful deference to Him who commands. They obey since they recognize His will for them as right and good. They understand that His every will is for the furtherance of His good and glorious purposes, inscrutable though they be. So also when Jesus was on earth He gave us His example of such hearty adoption of God's will as the pattern He would follow, knowing it as that of His Father, as good, and as for the welfare of the Kingdom.

When we pray, "Thy will be done on earth as it is in heaven," we are to recognize the heavenly order as the pattern which we choose. Christ's declaration, "I have come to do the will of Him that sent me," must be the ideal for every kingdom citizen. The deeds of the angels are in behalf of the heirs of salvation which also becomes a working objective for God's people.

We have then in offering this petition an ideal which is not an attenuated wish. It is a living ideal—actualized in heaven above and necessary now in the world below. Speaking of living ideals I appreciate that many people lift their eyebrows, and they do so either because of a spirit of sophistication or because they have had their hopes shattered. It is sad that so many can seemingly pretend a sympathetic understanding when men speak of their disillusionment. I believe that disillusionment has become for many an idol. Let me say that when people presume themselves disillusioned as to matters of religion, they are usually under a tragic illusion, even though they presume the very opposite. They have lost faith. Not disillusionment but faithlessness is the analysis of their trouble. Obedience as the angels render it is an ideal for us. The order of heaven with its perfection, its blissful harmony, and its God-glorifying movements is a reality. Its blessedness lies in the full harmony of all with the holy God. The Christian seeing the disorder in the earth can well learn to appreciate the words of John when he had seen the heavens open and said, "Amen, even so come, Lord Jesus." At the same time he knows the secret of heavenly blessedness which is perfect harmony with God and takes that as his goal. His life and every avenue of his relationships shall be a reaching for the goal of harmony with God in thought and deed. Following that gleam he will live nobly amongst men and usefully for God. It will be the secret of his joy, it will be the strength in his trials, and it will whet his desires for that final day

when sin shall be no more and he too shall be with
the angels and the saints of God in perfect harmony
with the Lord of all.

HEARTY COMMITMENT

But now we must consider also the hearty commitment involved in this prayer. Recently a Southern
preacher came to Grand Rapids to speak at a Calvinistic
Conference. When he saw the churches, the schools,
the college and seminary, and all the interest of our
people in the practical outworking of Calvinism, he
was amazed, and said, "You people here really mean
it when you call yourselves Calvinists." That might be
taken as a compliment, but it is also a commentary on
much American Christianity. Many don't mean it sincerely enough to carry out their religion into life. Now
we cannot say, "Thy will be done as in heaven" unless
we mean it. To mean it means a hearty commitment
to that will. Such commitment involves personal surrender. None less than our Saviour surrendered Himself
to the Father's will. If we would follow after Him we
too must begin with that personal surrender.

Someone has said, "The will is character in action."
Certainly we can affirm the truth of this statement as
to God. His character is ever evident in His will, but
this is also true of ourselves. That may startle us some-
what to be told our deeds are an expression of character. But, the new-born man is re-created. He receives
not just some blessed promises; he receives a calling
and a duty to fulfill. The slogan, "God wills it" becomes directive in his life with the result that his place
in life too contributes to the furtherance of God's
Kingdom. Our lives are often cluttered up with numerous immediate tasks and duties, but we are to remember

continually that the coming of God's Kingdom is our great interest, the furtherance of that kingdom our duty, and the doing of God's will our method of action.

The spirit of this suppliant is well expressed in the words we so often sing:

Take my life and let it be Consecrated, Lord, to Thee.
Take my moments and my days, Let them flow in endless praise.
Take my will and make it Thine; It shall be no longer mine.
Take my heart, it is Thine own; It shall be Thy royal throne.
Take my love; my Lord, I pour At thy feet its treasure store.
Take myself, and I will be Ever, only, all for Thee.

L

Fiftieth Lord's Day

THE MODEL PRAYER FOR EARTHLY NEEDS

Rev. Lubbertus Oostendorp

Scripture Reading: Matthew 6:24-39   *Text:* Matthew 6:11

WHENCE COME WARS? Come they not from your lusts? Ye lust, and have not! How true of the great World War II are these profound words of James. Germany's cry for *Lebensraum* is really a cry for bread. "Asia for the Asiatics" may simply be interpreted as the voice of Japan saying: "Give us the wealth of the world's greatest continent. Give it, or else we'll take it." Let us confess, however, that all nations manifest something of the same spirit. Behind every imperialism, every nationalism, capitalism and communism, stands the exalted human heart which says: "We must have economic security. We want wealth. We shall have it even if we must fight." Small wonder that the ceaseless appetite for more and more abundance should cause strife. Because of human unbelief and greed, the price of bread is blood.

We may say, therefore, that all men cry for bread. But only the true Christian prays for his needs. The world turns to Mars and Mammon. It says, "We will *force* the earth, the sea and the air to yield their wealth. If these be not enough, we have but to snatch the crusts from the bruised hands of our conquered fellow-men."

How different is the spirit of Christ! He gathers His humble disciples about Him and in one beautiful sentence teaches them the folly of the world's endless toil. Bread is not everything. Nor is it won by ingenious tools or death-spitting tanks. God giveth bread. While Caesars and Hitlers fight for bread and Shylocks cheat for gain, the Christians humbly pray for all their needs.

In this Model Prayer, Jesus teaches us the place, limits and confidence of the Christian's prayer for bread. As we consider Christ's model prayer for earthly needs, let us view it from these three angles: its integral place in Christian prayer; its modest request; and its confident approach.

There are good reasons for considering the proper place of the fourth petition. Undoubtedly, many of us recall memorizing lists of facts or names in school. Invariably, we'd ask whether it was necessary to know them "in the right order." If, as students of the Christ, we should ask the Master some such question about the six petitions of the Lord's Prayer, He would reply: "Most certainly, you must learn them in order. Each petition is important. You may not omit any one of them. And each has its proper place, the exact emphasis I have given it."

Why do we learn the Lord's Prayer anyway? Or rather, let me ask, how should we learn it? Who really knows this beautiful prayer? Millions of people can recite it by heart. But this is not enough. You cannot *pray* by heart. That can only be done *from* the heart. And here lies the significance of the order of the requests. You may be able to rush through the Lord's

Prayer in a very few seconds. Or perhaps you can repeat it in ten languages; and still you may not really *know* it at all. There's only one language which counts in prayer—the language of the heart.

Physical needs have a place in our hearts. Of this there can be no doubt. Prayer is the heart's sincere desire. Petition is the honest expression of what we feel. Jesus teaches us that when the heart, the regenerate heart of a true believer, speaks its own language it must cry out to God: "Give, O Heavenly Father, give bread!" When you and I pray as we should, according to the Model Prayer, we dare not omit the fourth petition. It must be there! But more than this, it must have its proper place. Let's consider each of these thoughts: Place and rightful place.

I already hear someone say: "Of course we must pray for our earthly blessings. Why, everybody does so!" But is it easy to give this petition room in our hearts? Let me assure you, there are few things harder of realization. The lips can easily say, "Give." Behind the closed eyes, however, a self-sufficient mind will still be echoing, "Need anyone give to me?" Human nature does not care to pray—least of all for shoes, meat, money.

Some time ago, I asked the Bible Class scholars how many of them would like to be beggars. Little Mary said: "I'd rather die than beg." "You'd never catch me holding a tin cup to anybody," added Jimmy. All spake thus, even as the steward in the parable: "To beg we are ashamed!" It was good of them to talk this way. But this thought came to me: How many of these children, or, for that matter, how many mortals will go through life with beggar's bowls held out to God? Jimmy says, "I'm strong"; and Johnny adds,

"I'm smart"; and Mary says, "I'm rich." How can this great Ego, the inflated human self, filled with earth's possession—how can that great "I" say: "Father, I plead, I beg, I pray for bread!" Only the humbled soul can say:

> Not to the strong is the battle,
> Not to the swift is the race,
> But to the true and the faithful
> Victory is promised through grace.

Always has it been hard to pray for bread. To ask each day for every need means recognizing God at every step of the way. Ever harder and harder becomes the inclusion of the fourth petition in prayer today. We are dealing with more than human pride. Today we are engulfed in materialism. The naturalism which denies that God *gives*—actually gives day by day each need—stifles every prayer, but most of all the plea for bread.

The whole spirit of our scientific age tends to eliminate all sense of immediate dependence upon God. In one of his last letters, Darwin (the father of evolution) tells us that as a boy he knelt piously each evening and asked God to take care of him, but in his old age he had reached a point where he could almost explain all things without the Almighty. Evolution had taken God out of the picture. There was no need for Him. All changes are by natural law. This was back in the latter part of the nineteenth century. Today, man has conquered the elements. It is science that will assure man of his bread. Vitamins and sulfanilamide for health! The doctor can cure anything! The machinist will find a way to solve every problem. We do not need God anymore. These are the thoughts of modern man!

And to a large extent, they are also the ideas of the so-called Christian. Some time ago at a meeting of ministers, the chairman asked whether anyone needed a tire. When one of the men replied that he could use a few, the clergyman replied: "Take your needs to the Lord." Everybody laughed. It was a good joke! What does God know or care about rubber shortage or tires for automobiles? God may feed the birds, but human beings must feed and clothe themselves. Besides, they are pretty well able to do so.

This, my fellow-Christians, is the godlessness of our age. Of it, one of my teachers was wont to say, "It is well-nigh impossible to make people see that God is interested in us!" Let us not imagine that we have escaped the evil of an independent world. Well may we ask ourselves whether we truly have given a place to the prayer for daily needs. Or have we too said: "We can take care of ourselves. We're doing pretty well." Oh, yes, we know that God hears prayers. But for all practical purposes, He is in the seventh heaven and we are on earth. How sorely then do we too need the reminder of Jesus: Your heavenly Father careth for you. Bread comes from Him. Give this thought a place in your prayer, and this prayer a place in your heart.

The prayer for physical needs has a place. To deny it is godlessness. But it must also have the rightful place. It is equally idolatrous to cry only for bread. Not first but after the plea for spiritual things, comes the request for bread. It is fitting that it should be so.

We are told, in a pretty fable, of two angels who went into the world to gather up the prayers of all men. As they returned heavenward, one carried a

41804

basket filled with pleas for shoes, houses, fields, automobiles and all earthly wants. The other came with a nearly empty basket. The spiritual prayers had been so few! There is a good point to the story. "Ye seek me," says Jesus, "for the loaves." Must man always be crying for the fleshpots of Egypt!

Need more be said of the tendency to give first place to earthly cares? We see the material standard often as the only measure of value. This is the great evil of the "social gospel." It is interested in a Christianity that first of all distributes bread. Thus do we find a popular writer like Pierre Van Paassen constantly complaining that Christianity has failed. And why has it been unsuccessful? Because it does not give enough bread! The means becomes the end. The purpose of the kingdom is to provide material well-being. It is very easy to turn things around. Well may we ask our own hearts whether they seek God for mammon or whether we ask for earthly needs to serve God! Jesus places first a petition for the spiritual, and again He ends with the glory of God. Between these great heavenly requests, He would have us include the cares of life. They must indeed have a place—but always a lesser, subservient position! Oh, never let this cry for bread be so important, so heart-filling, that it becomes all our prayer!

Thus have we considered the place given the fourth petition in the Model Prayer and in the language of the heart. We must turn to the second thought: The modest request. Modesty is apparent in every word. Not timidity or shyness but a genuine humility radiates from each expression. There is modesty in the term "bread"; in the idea of "daily" bread; in the inclusive "us"; and finally in the tone of simple dependence.

Bread! Nourishment, shelter, clothes, money and many more things are included in one word. Bread is the staff of life. As such, it represents all earthly needs. But it does so in the language of faith. The Gentiles think to be heard for the multiplicity of askings. They would help God discover what they need. You and I must not speak thus, for the Father knoweth our needs. Certainly, we may ask God for particulars. The rule must be the essential things, the central thought. This is the language of faith. May it ever be the modest language of our humble hearts! We will pray for bread. For Baby Jean, or sickly Jim, or hard-working Tom—O Lord, for all of these—Thou knowest what bread is! Give bread!

"How much?" you ask. Enough for today. Who but Jesus could have expressed so beautifully the limits of the Christian's physical desires? Our Lord here condemns much in our lives. The inflated standard of living which claims every luxury as a need cannot come under daily bread. I do not say that Jesus cuts ice cream and pie from the menu and leaves us with the monk's bowl of dried peas. We are surrounded with abundance. Let us enjoy it! But we may not say: "Lord give me more, more, more!"

On the other hand, this modest phrase leaves room for all the variety of needs, without giving place to anxiety or human self-sufficiency. The limit is *today*. Each day we need God's care. An infant may need only its few ounces of milk. The growing boy has more appetite than Grandmother who sits in her corner and eats as little as a bird. A common laborer, no doubt, has less need than the President of the United States. Jesus is not narrow. He does not count out pennies. He merely says: "Be modest. Be content for today.

If thy needs be few, God knows. If they be many, He who feeds countless sparrows will feed thee, too."

A prayer for daily bread is a modest prayer. Jesus makes it still more humble by saying "us." No matter how we limit the amount, if we continue always to say "give *me*," we miss the spirit of Christ. The heart that is selfish is also immodest. It is not in the proper attitude for this prayer.

What would you think of a man who would jump overboard in midocean and try to swim to shore? He would be most foolish. Still, this is what the man who does not pray is trying to do. He thinks to win his own way, little realizing his dependence. Equally absurd would be the passenger who would say: "Captain, throw all the other travelers overboard. I want to ride the ship alone!" That's what the man does who says *"me"* instead of *"us."* And how often, in this request, our actions contradict our words. Though we prattle about "us," we think and love only "me." Harsh international treaties which would reduce whole peoples to poverty say, "Give me." The capitalist who knows only the profit motive says: "Give me." The laborer who works only to beat his employer shouts, "Give me." The farmer who views his growing wheat and thinks of it only in terms of jingling coin, and never once of all the hungry mouths it feeds, may be saying something about "us," but isn't he really praying, "Give me"? Oh, how selfish, how narrow, how foolish we are! Teach thy servants, gracious Lord, in the days of egotism to pray humbly, sincerely: "Give us."[2]

If our hearts can truly echo each word of this prayer which our lips so readily learn, then truly will our petition be trusting and modest. It will leave to

God the amount of our needs. Least of all will it be a selfish prayer. Well may we ask ourselves: "Have we learned the beauty of those words by humbly leaving all to the Father who careth for us?"

We have considered the place of this petition and its modest request. There remains one important thought: Its confident approach. Confidence characterizes every petition of the Lord's Prayer. It is, however, particularly significant in the prayer for daily needs. There is something about the way Jesus says "Give" that strikes us. The doubtful beggar may say "Please." Perhaps he will be heard because of his sugary words! The bold parasite would command and cry: "I want." Jesus confidently says: "Give." "The Lord knows you well. He will care for you. He can do so, being Almighty God. He will do so as a loving Father." These are the thoughts which one reads behind the simple words.

Yes, indeed, God is able. He feeds the sparrows, cares for the hairs of your head. Let there be no doubt in prayer. James tells us that "we have not, though asking, because we ask amiss." Elijah prayed earnestly: first to shut up the heavens, and then for rain. He was heard because he knew God would hear him. So, too, all unbelief is ruled out of the heart that once really says: "Give, O God, give bread."

Certainly God is willing to care for us. If the very lilies bloom by His loving care, "how much more will He care for you, O ye of little faith." The Christian remembers in each petition that he is talking to his Father, and though that Father be in heaven, He does not give stones for bread, nor scorpions for fishes. He will—yea, I know He will—care for us! Thus can we come, in full assurance laying all our needs before Him.

It may be hard, when prosperity smothers prayer, to say, "Give bread." In life's busy conflict the battle does seem to be to the strong. Science, invention and human might do appear to wrest bread from the earth. But for you and me there remains the Hand, the Invisible Power, which really provides.

> Unless the Lord the house shall build,
> The weary builders toil in vain;
> Unless the Lord the city shield,
> The guards a useless watch maintain.
>
> In vain you rise ere morning break,
> And late your nightly vigils keep,
> And of the bread of toil partake,
> God gives to His beloved sleep.

Let us not divorce bread and God, nor omit this prayer from our hearts. Nor dare we make bread our "God," but modestly and humbly we shall seek each need from Him who knoweth what is best for us. And if sometimes earth seems far from God and only by faith we can pray, then know that soon the day will dawn when we shall no longer hunger nor thirst. Then shall we eat the bread of life forevermore.

LI

Fifty-First Lord's Day

THE REDISCOVERY OF FORGIVENESS

REV. RICHARD C. OUDERSLUYS

Scripture Reading: Matt. 18:21-35   *Text:* Matt. 6:12

THE FIFTH PETITION of the Lord's Prayer brings everyone of us to a solemn pause. At this point the Lord's Prayer becomes unmistakably crucial in its demand for Christian understanding and sincerity. That Jesus Himself considered this petition one of crucial importance, is indicated by the fact that He returned to further discuss it. Of all the topics in the Prayer, this is the only one which Jesus took up a second time and enlarged upon. This, in itself, speaks for the importance of the fifth petition.

In our day of fuller Christian revelation it is easier to understand why Jesus emphasized the fifth petition. It deals with one of the most central and distinctive truths of the Christian gospel—the truth of forgiveness. It is a truth which occupied a large place in the teaching of Jesus Christ; and necessarily so, because He came into the world with the claim to have power under God to forgive sins. It is a truth which has continued to occupy a large place in Christian experience, because no one can rightly claim to be Christian unless he has received the forgiveness of sins. And the truth of forgiveness has always been the secret of the triumph of Christianity in its every age of power and prestige.

Today, however, in our modern welter of confused thought and belief, the truth of forgiveness has become sadly obscured. We notice a strange difference between the popular view and Christ's view of forgiveness. Christ viewed the fifth petition as cardinal and crucial. Popular Christianity does not profess to view the petition in this light. Christ taught that the fifth petition was difficult and demanding. We seem to find it easy to pray; we repeat it casually, and even glibly. Christ said that the praying of this petition was impossible for those who do not possess the forgiving spirit. We do not seem to see any strangely forbidding condition in this petition, and pray for forgiveness regardless of whether or not we are forgiving.

This strange difference between Christ's view of forgiveness and our own indicates that we have failed properly to understand the mind of Christ concerning this great truth. Forgiveness should mean to us what it so evidently meant to Christ—a truth of great saving, controlling and demanding power. It is needful that we recapture this truth of forgiveness for our day. We need to rediscover its personal and social significance. It is time that we face squarely the assertion of Jesus that Divine forgiveness and human willingness to forgive are inseparable. *Our world needs, as never before, the rediscovery of the glorious truth of Divine forgiveness, and its vital relation to human forgiveness.*

I. The Glorious Truth of Divine Forgiveness

The fifth petition of the Lord's Prayer directs our minds, in the first place, to the glorious truth of Divine forgiveness. Jesus teaches us to pray, "Father, forgive us our debts." In authorizing the praying of this petition, Jesus did not stop to discuss the propriety or the rightfulness of forgiveness. And at no time in His life did Jesus ever try to convince people that forgiveness was a properly moral or perfectly real thing. Jesus assumed the necessity, the rightfulness and the realness of forgiveness. Jesus knew that if the human mind were honest and the conscience alert, the need for forgiveness would be self-evident. And He likewise knew that if minds were not honest, and consciences were not alert, it would be futile to argue men into believing that they were sinners. So with unerring wisdom and characteristic boldness, Jesus penetrated at once to the core of human difficulty. He assumed the fact of sin, and proceeded to teach men to pray for the forgiveness of their sins. Jesus was confident that honest souls would be able to see and appreciate the glory and the wonder of Divine forgiveness. And honest souls in every age do see its wonder and glory.

For one thing, we see that the wonder and glory of God's forgiveness lies in the measure of its *necessity*. Divine forgiveness addresses itself to what is so clearly our need—release from the accusing weight of our sins. When we are honest with ourselves, we know ourselves as sinners. Evidence of sin bears in upon us from all sides. Crime waves, violence, social injustice, economic tyranny—what is all of this but sin? When people exploit one another for selfish purposes, this is sin! When people sell one another into war and bloodshed for the sake of profit, this, too, is sin—sin as scarlet as the blood that flows from the wounds of war. However, for evidence of sin we do not need to refer to extreme instances of evil. The greatest proof of our sinfulness lies in the condemnation that proceeds from our own hearts. "Conscience doth make cowards of us all." We carry around with us a never-diminishing sense of guilt—a guilt that cleaves to us night and day. We have a painful consciousness of separation from God, who is our true life. In the words of our Catechism, we are painfully aware of the weight of *"our transgressions and the evil which always cleaves to us."*

> None, O Lord, have perfect rest,
>   For none are wholly free from sin;
> And they who fain would serve Thee best
>   Are conscious most of wrong within.

This sense of personal guilt and unworthiness is immeasurably increased by the life and presence of Jesus Christ. His life and teaching, passion and death, make our sinfulness more readily apparent—and more keenly felt. Facing Christ, the honest soul cries out, "Depart from me, for I am a sinful man, O Lord!" Especially when our lives stand in the presence of Jesus do we feel that there is something within us that needs forgiveness. The wonder and glory of Divine forgiveness lies in the measure of its necessity. The forgiveness which God offers us in His Son, Jesus Christ, does not belittle the fact of sin. The effect of Christ's mission was to intensify and deepen our consciousness of sin and our need of forgiveness.

The wonder of God's forgiveness looms even more magnificent when we consider the measure of its *reality*. We can pray God to forgive us our sins, because we are confident that forgiveness awaits us. And it is a very real forgiveness. Christ's mission was not only to increase and intensify our sense of sin. His mission was also one of deliverance and forgiveness. An unbroken chain of Christian witnesses from the first Christian century down to this present century, declares the realness and effectualness of Divine forgiveness. Souls once living under the weight of an accusing conscience find their burden lifted. They find a joy and peace that were formerly impossible to them. They find within them a new power that makes them live like the sons of God. Upon receiving forgiveness, they find life new and promising. No longer do they feel alienated and separated from God. Trusting God's power to forgive and to destroy sin, they find sin forgiven and destroyed.

The wonder of Divine forgiveness lies in what it can do to the forgiven soul, and in what it can make the forgiven soul do. It removes the burden of guilt from the soul. It produces lives of stimulating goodness and moral progress. It effects that glorious sense of being alive. It makes all things new. Paul, better than anyone else, describes the realness of forgiveness when he says, "And you, being dead in your sins, hath he quickened together with him, having forgiven you all trespasses."

The wonder and glory of God's forgiveness is best revealed in the measure of its infinite cost and worth. The forgiveness which God gives to men is not a cheap nor easy thing. Forgiveness is never cheap nor easy. We know this from our own limited experience of forgiveness. In both God and man, it is always bought with a great price. We shall never rightly appreciate the glory of God's forgiveness until we are impressed with the agony of its cost.

In order to properly pray this fifth petition of the Lord's Prayer, we must bring to it a Christian understanding. We must pray this petition in the light of the entire New Testament teaching about forgiveness. There is no mention in this petition of the only Christian ground for forgiveness, namely, the atonement of Jesus Christ. The disciples would hardly have been able to understand such a reference before Christ's death. After the death and resurrection of Jesus Christ, the disciples saw clearly how it was possible for God to forgive sins. They realized that forgiveness of sins was available because of the sacrifice and death of Jesus Christ. Our Catechism in this connection very fittingly reminds us of this same truth when it bids us pray God that "He be pleased, for the sake of Christ's blood, not to impute to us, miserable sinners, any of our transgressions."

The sacrifice and death of Jesus Christ help us to understand God's forgiveness. They speak to us of what it cost God to forgive sin. They tell us that God's forgiveness of sin is not a mere overlooking of sin. His forgiveness is not cheap nor easy. It is in harmony with His Divine justice and holiness. It is in harmony with the moral law which governs our world. It is a forgiveness which commands respect and gratitude. In Christ, sin was punished and justice satisfied. God pardons sin, but at great cost to Himself. In the cross of Christ, sin was condemned, sin was conquered and forgiveness made possible. And in all of this God Himself suffered in the person of His only-begotten Son. In praying God to forgive us our debts, we ought always to remember Calvary.

> We may not know, we cannot tell
>   What pains He had to bear;
> But we believe it was for us,
>   He hung and suffered there.

He died that we might be forgiven;
He died to make us good,
That we might go at last to heaven,
Saved by His precious blood.

In our day, we need to rediscover this wonder and glory of Divine forgiveness. We need to discover how vitally this truth speaks to our human need. We need to discover the convincing realness of forgiveness. We need to discover anew the priceless and immeasurable dignity and worth of the forgiveness which comes to us through the passion and death of Jesus Christ.

Rediscovering these truths, we will find that Divine forgiveness becomes more meaningful for us. It is the failure to discover the true nature of forgiveness that often brings its truth into disrepute. Forgiveness is not to be had for walking down a sawdust trail or shaking a preacher's hand. Forgiveness does not mean that God winks at sin and merely overlooks it. If Bernard Shaw, our great modern British critic, had understood forgiveness in the light of the cross, he would not have said, "Forgiveness is a beggar's refuge. We must pay our debts."

Many people have come to feel that forgiveness is unreal and unnecessary, because so often it has been presented in a cheap, flippant fashion. But when properly understood, what a glorious truth it is for human souls. The sight of God's Son suffering for our sins breaks us down and melts us into repentance. It stirs us to a life of moving gratitude and goodness. To appreciate the glorious truth of Divine forgiveness, we must remember, as our Catechism suggests, that it pleases God, for the sake of Christ's blood, not to impute to us poor sinners our transgressions nor that depravity which always cleaves to us.

II. Its Vital Relation to Human Forgiveness

We have asserted our need for rediscovering the glory of Divine forgiveness. But our rediscovery of forgiveness should not stop at this point. Jesus did not stop when He said, *"Forgive us our debts."* He proceeded to say, *"even as we forgive our debtors."* We must therefore rediscover also the vital relation between Divine forgiveness and human forgiveness. Let this fact never escape us: Jesus asserted and taught a vital relationship between God's forgiveness of our sins and our forgiveness of those who sin against us. And lest this significant relationship escape our notice, Jesus purposely returned and emphasized it by declaring, *"If ye forgive men their trespasses, your heavenly Father will also forgive you: But if ye forgive not men their trespasses, neither will your Father forgive your trespasses."* Our Catechism rightly reminds us that we should pray God to forgive us our transgressions and ever-present depravity, *"as we also find this witness of Thy grace in us that it is our full purpose heartily to forgive our neighbor."* We are forbidden to seek Divine forgiveness apart from human forgiveness. If we would be forgiven, we must forgive.

Now, what did Jesus mean when He taught us to pray, *"Forgive us our debts, as we also have forgiven our debtors"?* What is the relation between Divine and human forgiveness? Certainly this relation is not one of *merit*. In praying this petition we do not ask God to forgive us our sins because we forgive those who sin against us. Our human forgiveness does not merit God's forgiveness. As we have already stated, the only ground of Divine forgiveness is the atonement of Jesus Christ. And certainly this relation is not one of *measure*. We do not ask God to forgive us our debts in the measure in which we forgive our debtors. The small, niggardly measure of man's forgiveness can never become the standard for God's forgiveness.

> For the love of God is broader,
> Than the measure of man's mind;
> And the heart of the Eternal
> Is most wonderfully kind.

The relation between Divine and human forgiveness is neither one of merit nor of measure. It is a relation of *possibility*. When we forgive others their trespasses, we make it possible for God to forgive us our trespasses. God's forgiveness is instant, and ready to pour itself into our lives, if we will open them to His forgiving love. But if we harbor within our hearts grudges and enmities, petty jealousies and hatreds against our fellow-men, these attitudes become spiritual obstacles to the entrance of God's love and forgiveness. When hatred, envy and malice take possession of the soul, they lock the door and bar the way to love and forgiveness. It lies in the very nature of forgiveness that it is possible only to those who are forgiving. When we clog the channels of our lives with enmities, spites and jealousies, we make it impossible for God's forgiveness to reach us.

The relation between Divine and human forgiveness may also be described as one of *sincerity*. To pray God to forgive us our debts without being willing to forgive those indebted to us is to be guilty of insincerity. The soul is perjured, damaged by such a prayer. How is it possible for one to ask for forgiveness with sincerity, when one denies to others forgiveness? And yet, there are many people who attempt this very thing. Many are under the delusion that they can stand in the searching presence of God—before whom all minds are as open books—and ask for pardon, while they themselves deny pardon to their fellow-men. This is one of the most damaging delusions of which the human soul is capable. The human soul cannot stand up under such insincerity. Insincerity perverts, deteriorates the soul. Insincerity kills the soul. The human soul is a wonderful thing. It can stand up under any number of life's pressures and strains. It can take pain, loss, disappointment, sorrow and even betrayal; but it cannot take continued insincerity.

It was for this reason that Jesus was so concerned about the man who came to offer a gift at the altar while he was still unreconciled to his brother. Jesus knew that he was perverting his very soul by such action. And Jesus said to that man and to all men, "Leave thy gift before the altar, and go thy way; first be reconciled to thy brother, and then come and offer thy gift." The sincerity of our plea for forgiveness is revealed by the forgiving spirit which we adopt toward others.

This relation between Divine and human forgiveness may be described further as one of *appreciation*. A person cannot have any real appreciation for God's forgiveness unless he knows what forgiveness means in his own life. To forgive others who deeply wrong us, to take the initiative and reach out to knit together old ties of friendship—this constitutes one of life's most painful and difficult tasks. And yet, one who has never been willing to do this can have but little appreciation of what he is asking of God. How vividly Jesus pressed home to the heart this truth in the parable of the Unmerciful Servant, which was read for our

Scripture. This servant owed his lord ten thousand talents, in other words, about two million dollars. A tremendous sum! An unpayable debt!

This is a sober reminder of our terrible indebtedness to God. We can never become morally or spiritually solvent before God. Our debt to Him is beyond our human ability to pay. And yet the lord forgave his servant the debt. And as Dr. George A. Buttrick in his brilliant book, *The Parables of Jesus,* says so discerningly, "The ten thousand talents describe not only our bankruptcy of soul before God, but also the measure of God's compassion. Ten thousand talents hints the dire cost of forgiveness that comes to us through Calvary's Cross." The lord forgave his servant the debt for he realized the man's inability to pay. The lord took the loss himself.

But then what happened? This same servant who had been so mercifully forgiven and pardoned went out and laid hold on a fellow-servant who owed him a hundred shillings, in other words, about twenty dollars. It was a debt that could have been paid. Twenty dollars was nothing compared to two million dollars. Yet, because his fellow-servant could not pay the twenty dollars upon demand, the servant became infuriated. He took him by the throat and, shaking him, roared, "Pay me what thou owest!" In heartless fury he commanded that the fellow-servant be thrown into prison. When the news of this strange transaction came to the ears of the lord, no wonder that he called his servant to account. No wonder he said to him, "Thou wicked servant. I forgave you all that debt because you so entreated me! Why did you not have mercy upon your fellow-servant, as I had mercy upon you?" And in righteous indignation the lord delivered the servant

into the hands of tormentors until he should pay all
that was due.

Dare we ask for Divine mercy when we refuse to
show human mercy? Dare we have the effrontery to
ask God to forgive us our two-million-dollar debt of
sin, and then refuse to forgive our neighbor his twenty-
dollar transgression? You would think it impossible;
but alas, there are those who attempt to do it. He who
refuses to forgive can have but little appreciation of
the forgiveness which he asks of God.

> We do pray for mercy; and that same prayer
> should teach us all to render the deeds of mercy.

It is imperative in our day that we rediscover the
vital connection between Divine and human forgiveness.
Our lives need to feel the force of Jesus' assertion that
these two forgiving acts are joined inseparably. We
cannot have a forgiveness of our personal sins apart
from a forgiving attitude. We cannot be smugly com-
placent about our favor with God when we are holding our fellow-men in disfavor. Too many Christian
people are trying to build their Christianity solely upon
their privileges and duties to God. Their acceptance
of the Christian gospel establishes for them but one
relationship—a relationship to God. Jesus asserted, and
the entire New Testament is united in declaring, that
the relationships of a Christian are twofold—a relationship to God, and a relationship to one's neighbor.

What a reflection it is on their Christianity when
those who claim to know something about forgiveness,
who claim to have received forgiveness under God,
still go about with unforgiving attitudes! What an
indictment against the Christian Church which is supposed to represent the "community of the forgiven"!

How is the world to be challenged and convinced of the reality of Divine forgiveness except by the forgiven and forgiving life of Christian people? The world will remain unconvinced, and will even smile at the truth of forgiveness, until Christian people demonstrate it in their lives. Why should people of the world believe in forgiveness of sins, when they so seldom meet with human sympathy, kindness and mercy? How can the word "forgiveness" have any meaning for them if they seldom, if ever, encounter forgiving attitudes in life?

Today, we stand in a world crisis! Suspicion and rivalry, greed and ambition are to be found in every quarter of the globe. Never before as a world have we been so keenly aware of "man's inhumanity to man." Never before has it been so apparent that "man is to man the sorest, surest ill." Modern industry ruthlessly throws millions of men into unemployment. Labor groups respond with secret and open hatred, oftentimes with violence. Our modern society seems indifferent or is powerless to remedy unfair inequalities, injustices and tyrannies. The old doctrine that might makes right is brought to its fullest expression in our day in the dictators who rule over Russia and Red China. Race prejudice has never been so evident as in the wave of anti-Semitism that has often swept European lands. We are not wholly free from it even in our own country. Even in the Church of Jesus Christ the fires of fairness and kindness often burn low. Nothing could serve better in our day than a rediscovery of the truth of forgiveness with its saving personal and social relations. A rediscovery of this forgiveness which makes men forgiving and loving would go a long way—yes, all the way—in solving our world difficulties.

And who are in a better position to make this rediscovery than Christian people? As Dr. H. R. Macintosh in his splendid book, *The Christian Experience of Forgiveness,* states so well: "The Church represents the community of the forgiven." That is, the Church stands for a people who claim forgiveness, who rejoice in forgiveness. Is not the Church, then, best fitted to demonstrate the power of forgiveness in the world? It is the Church that makes the truth of forgiveness credible to the world. The conviction that God forgives sins will never rise in the hearts of men unless they see the forgiven actually forgiving. No other group of people hold in their hands—so evidently—the remedy for the ills of our world as do those who have been pardoned of God through Jesus Christ. The pardoned will pardon. The forgiven and loved will forgive and love.

The fifth petition of the Lord's Prayer lays upon us all a great mission. Leaving the sanctuary this (morning), it must be with malice, envy and hatred left behind, or we shall stand indicted before God even as the Unmerciful Servant. This morning we must leave on a new mission of love and forgiveness. If it is true that we are the children of God through His forgiveness, then we must live like brothers and sisters, and forgive. We cannot be *sons,* if we are not willing to be *brothers!* Not only our prayer-life, but our entire life must be fitted to the truth of this fifth petition which we have studied together this hour.

If we do not, how shall we ever face that Christ

who, on an unjust cross, with undeserved nails in His hands and feet, still prayed, saying, "Father, forgive them for they know not what they do"? This is the word of our Christ: "Pray ye after this manner: *Father, forgive us our debts as we forgive our debtors.*"

LII

Fifty-Second Lord's Day

THE CONCLUDING PETITION AND THE DOXOLOGY OF THE LORD'S PRAYER

REV. MARTIN MONSMA

Scripture Reading: Ephesians 6   *Text:* Matt. 6:13

MAN CANNOT HAVE genuine joy in life and peace of heart except he find it in God through Christ. Through Him, our crucified Redeemer who purchased our pardon, the believer can say: "My soul shall be joyful in my God" (Isa. 61:10). Through Him the believer will experience repeatedly that "light is sown for the righteous, and gladness for the upright in heart" (Ps. 97:11). When trials and sore afflictions are his he may confidently assert: "Though I walk in the midst of trouble, thou wilt revive me" (Ps. 138:7). And even in the most trying dangers of life he may triumphantly exclaim: "Yea, though I walk through the valley of the shadow of death, I will fear no evil: for thou art with me" (Ps. 23:4).

But he who would infer from all this that the way of a Christian in this life is like a primrose path of glory and ease, would misjudge badly.

Consider that every believer is saved for service. He is called out of darkness and into God's marvelous light in order that he should show forth the excellencies of God (I Peter 2:9). He is a soldier in the army of the living God. A constant warfare is his. And, oh, what a warfare! Listen to the Spirit's testimony through Paul: "For we wrestle not against flesh and blood, but against principalities, against powers, against the rulers of the darkness of this world, against spiritual wickedness in high places" (Eph. 6:12).

Moreover, the disappointments of life are often sore trials for the believer. Self-denial and conflict are often irksome. Daily marches and constant combat in the service of God often become tiresome.

Jesus knew all this full well. Consequently He taught us to pray: "Bring us not into temptation, but deliver us from the evil one."

This sixth petition of the Lord's Prayer requires our first and primary attention in this sermon.

He who utters the Lord's Prayer thoughtfully and sincerely thereby confesses that there are certain enemies which oppose him constantly, plotting and attempting his ruin. For rest assured, in this beautiful prayer, composed by Christ Himself, there is not so much as one meaningless syllable. Every phrase and petition in it is founded upon realities and truths that allow of no questioning. Now, in this prayer our Lord teaches us specifically to pray against the Evil One and his temptations. This Evil One together with his agents and agencies, our Catechism denotes as our sworn enemies—enemies that are as it were bound by a hellish oath to plot and attempt our spiritual destruction.

Satan is that fallen archangel who was the leader of those "angels which kept not their first estate, but left their own habitation" (Jude 6). He is now the arch-demon and arch-plotter against God and man. All his spiritual ability and ingenuity with which he once served and glorified God, he now uses, as much as he is able, against God and His handiwork. His cunning craftiness, wicked wiles and poisoned arrows are directed especially against the children of God, whom God is redeeming out of this world of sin and delivering from the devil's dominion. For note how God admonishes us that "Satan himself is transformed into an angel of light" (II Cor. 11:14). And Christ warned His followers of the fact that "there shall arise false Christs, and false prophets, and shall shew great signs and wonders; insomuch that, if it were possible, they shall deceive the very elect" (Matt. 24:24). And again He testifies through Paul: "Put on the whole armor of God, that ye may be able to stand against the wiles of the devil" (Eph. 6:11).

Now it is to be expected that the unbeliever of this twentieth century, this age of mechanical advancement and marvelous inventions, often serving only self and sin, recognizes no spiritual dangers. He denies their reality, for he denies the very existence of the devil. And let no one imagine that these modern Sadducees are only among the rank and file of the people who have not enjoyed a higher education. To the contrary, the leaders of these blind leaders of the blind often wear caps and gowns and even hold influential pastorates.

Many of these sneer at the very thought of a devil. Belief in his existence and activity they call nonsense. Let us be sure that nothing could please this monster of wickedness more. It gives him an excellent opportunity to work under cover.

How sad this folly and blindness of unbelief! May we constantly pray for the opening of the eyes of the blind, and may we be found loyal to our task as witnesses of God's truth. But that the world of unbelief should disbelieve the reality of the devil and his angels and should fail to heed the fearful spiritual dangers to which men stand exposed, is after all to be expected.

But neither do we Christians of this age live in the realization of our constant spiritual dangers. In this day of restless speed, material preoccupation, social Christianity and worldly-mindedness, we tend to spiritual shallowness. And consequently the spiritual foes of former days against whom Christ teaches His disciples to pray, lurk beneath the surface of our lives even more freely and more numerously. This being true, surely we may well pray: "Bring us not into temptation, but deliver us from the evil one."

"Deliver us from the evil one." Note well that Christ does not merely teach us to pray against certain contrary circumstances called "evil." Not at all. He teaches us to pray for deliverance from the very person of the Evil One. This fact should be outstanding in our minds. The devil is our personal enemy. He is our adversary, our cruel opponent; for thus God speaks concerning him: "Be sober, be vigilant; because your adversary the devil, as a roaring lion, walketh about, seeking whom he may devour" (I Peter 5:8).

But how does the devil work? What is his program and range of activity? How does he endeavor to translate his enmity against us into deeds of destruction?

The Scriptures teach that the evil spirits exert certain influences upon men. These influences are, of course, always for evil. Concerning King Saul we read that an evil spirit from Jehovah troubled him, moved him to raging anger and deeds of violence (I Samuel 16:18).

Satan is said to have entered Judas Iscariot. This is not to be identified with the demon possession of Jesus' day, as a result of which the victims became helpless and irresponsible. Judas so yielded himself to his love for money and temporal glory that Satan, as it were, took complete possession of him and used him as a willing tool for his wicked schemes. The sin of Ananias and Sapphira was their own sin. The apostle holds them to strict accountability; yet Satan moved them to sin; for we read: "Ananias, why hath Satan filled thine heart to lie to the Holy Ghost?" (Acts 5:3). David, the man after God's own heart, was moved by Satan to number Israel. Christians are warned by Paul not to give place to the devil (Eph. 4:27), and James assures us, "Resist the devil, and he will flee from you" (James 4:7). Beyond a doubt, the devil and his evil angels can exert certain spiritual influences over us. That such demoniac influences exist is clearly taught in both the Old and the New Testament.

Just how the evil spirits establish their contacts with us and operate within us, none can say. Let us remember in this connection that much of the spiritual realm lies far beyond our direct observation and defies all analysis. All we can say is that Satan finds his contact in the natural depravity of our nature and that he operates especially in connection with those personal weaknesses and evil tendencies which are prominent in our lives. He works through such sinful tendencies as pride, selfishness, avarice, lust and anger. If the tendency to sinful pride and haughtiness be outstanding in your heart, he will cater to it through the flattery of the world, and thus endeavor to make you worldly and vain. If the weeds of selfishness seem to grow easily in your heart, he will seek to make self-denial appear unpleasant and unnecessary. If avarice be your peculiar sin, he will tempt you to center your first thoughts on money and possessions, to the hurt of your spiritual life and the progress of God's kingdom. If the beast of carnal lusts readily raises its head within your bosom, he will endeavor to center your thoughts on things carnal and even paint the sins of lusts as innocent and attractive things. If in anger you easily flare up at the least provocation, he will be sure to provoke you to anger repeatedly. In a sly, cunning, hidden way he will seek to cast down the bars to sin in your heart and life and block the Spirit's sanctifying activity within you.

Parents, let us remember at this point that although we cannot bind Satan into inactivity as far as our children are concerned, we can safeguard them against many of his agencies and tools, such as godless instruction, worldly companions, modernistic novels, suggestive and filthy magazines and radio nonsense. Let us constantly warn our children, by word and deed, against all that is "of the world." For the Bible does not merely speak of Satan as a tempter who entices to sin, but as a fowler who sets his snares with cunning craft, unnoticed by his intended victims, and as one who sows the evil seed of tares in the wheat fields of our hearts under cover of night, unseen and unmolested.

Worldly men, in their vanity and fool-hardiness, often describe Satan as a weird, gruesome-looking creature, with hoofs and horns, armed with a barbed fork, garbed in glaring red. Well might we wish that the devil would so appear on our streets and in our homes, in our synagogues and in our haunts of sinful pleasure!

Our fathers used to speak also of "Satanic assaults."

Our Catechism here also speaks of them. By Satanic assaults our fathers meant the devil's attacks upon our spiritual poise and our peace of heart.

Sometimes believers find that evil thoughts seem to arise in their hearts instantaneously and apparently without provocation. Even thoughts of blasphemy and hatred toward God will suddenly, and as it seems, immediately, come up within us to disturb our peace— perhaps even while we are engaged in prayer. These dreadful experiences were for our forefathers not only a token of our natural depravity; they also linked them with the devil's activity and attributed them to direct assaults on the part of the Evil One. Furthermore, thoughts of doubt and unbelief pertaining to God or His Christ sometimes vex the believer and disturb his peace of heart and mind, until prayer and reflection cause them to vanish as quickly as they came. Again, serious doubt and anxious fear of heart about his own state of grace sometimes come upon the believer. He fears that he is not a child of God but a son of the devil still. His sins seem to loom up before him, high as a towering mountain; his hope of forgiveness and salvation, if at all present, is comparable only to a faint glimmer.

Now to be sure, much of this finds its counterpart in our everyday experiences. Psychologically considered, some of these experiences are not so mysterious as might appear at first glance. And considered in the light of God's revelation pertaining to our partial knowledge of God and our limited comprehension of things Divine, and of what it teaches about the depravity of our hearts, the heinousness of sin, and man's absolute unworthiness of salvation, these experiences should not surprise us. Nevertheless, the Scriptures speak with such clearness regarding the influence and scope of the work of the demons that it is not without warrant that these fearful conflicts are ascribed to the activity of Satan.

Doubtless it is true that God often permits these seasons of spiritual depression and conflict to come upon us because we have forsaken Him. We may believe that He often withdraws Himself and His grace from our consciousness and thus exposes us to the devil's assaults in order to awaken us from our spiritual stupor, or to recall us from our sin and our devotion to the things of earth.

Do we not sing even today with David of old:

> While I kept guilty silence
>   My strength was spent with grief,
> Thy hand was heavy on me,
>   My soul found no relief (Ps. 32).

And do not believers today sometimes find occasion to complain in bitterness of soul: "O my God, I cry in the daytime, but thou hearest not; and in the night season, and am not silent"? (Ps. 22). And do we never find occasion to plead: "Take not thy holy Spirit from me. Restore unto me the joy of thy salvation"? (Ps. 51). Well may we all heed the words of our Saviour: "Watch and pray, that ye enter not into temptation" (Matt. 26:41), and of Paul: "Let him that thinketh he standeth take heed lest he fall" (I Cor. 10:12).

But our Catechism would not have us think only of the devil and his subordinate evil spirits, as we pray: "And bring us not into temptation, but deliver us from the evil one." Our fathers held that Christ was also thinking of the world of sin in which we live and of our sinful inclinations, when he gave the words of this prayer.

Why should the world be classified as a sworn enemy of God's people? Is it not God's own handiwork? And is it not still His and the object of His constant love and care? Yes indeed, for God assures us: "The world is mine and the fulness thereof" (Ps. 50: 12). But the word "world" is often used in Scripture to designate the sinful inhabitants of the world, or the forces of darkness which oppose God and His people. Thus Jesus uses the word in John 15:19: "If ye were of the world, the world would love his own: but because ye are not of the world, but I have chosen you out of the world, therefore the world hateth you."

Now the world, in this evil sense, is under the dominion of Satan, by God's permission, and Satan uses this dominion against us in numerous ways. Thus, for example, he uses men and women to tempt us, the pleasures of sin to entice us and the appeal of riches to allure us.

First, the children of the world often entice us to sin. In the days of the apostles many walked in lasciviousness, lusts, winebibbings, revelings and carousings. They thought it strange that the believers would not join them in the same excess of riot, and they spoke evil of the Christians because they refused to join them (I Peter 4:4). Today it is the same story. Young people especially should remember this. By word and example and friendly invitation the unbelievers will invite God's covenant people to join them in their worldly pleasures.

Now, if the enticement would always come from those that have gone to the limit of iniquity, like the pagans of Peter's day, the danger would not be so great.

For the revelries and carousings of the world repel, at first, even our natural sensibilities. But we should beware especially of enticements and friendly invitations to so-called "good shows," "innocent" card parties, "social" dances, the carnivals, fairs, amusement parks and parties at which evil, though predominant, is nevertheless mixed with good. Let us ever beware of the devil's sugar-coated pills of poison.

We should, moreover, make friends with God's people and not with those whose portion is here below. Let us remember the dire results which friendships between the Church and the world always have had for the Church. Think of the children of Seth and the children of Cain. God's people must be separate. That is God's will. "Have no fellowship with the unfruitful works of darkness," says the Lord (Eph. 5:11). And again: "Be not unequally yoked together with unbelievers: for what fellowship hath righteousness with unrighteousness? and what communion hath light with darkness? . . . or what part hath he that believeth with an infidel?" (II Cor. 6:14, 15).

Twentieth-century Christianity is weak in numerous ways. One is, beyond a doubt, that it lacks distinctiveness. All too many are compromising with the world and its hollow, sinful pleasures—also, sad to say, some who belong to our Reformed groups. Might not the apostle James say to us: "Ye adulterers and adulteresses, know ye not that the friendship of the world is enmity with God?" (James 4:4). And have not many, also of this day, made a god out of their gold? Material possessions and luxuries and social standing have polluted the blood-stream of vital Christianity. The Church of God is suffering from spiritual pernicious anemia by reason of worldly-mindedness and related evils. Many of God's children do not labor fervently for the coming of God's Kingdom in their hearts and homes because they have imbibed too long and too freely from the cup of self-centered, materialistic, pleasure-loving living!

Would to God that we might all remember the admonition which God directs to us, in words solemn and clear: "Love not the world, neither the things that are in the world. If any man love the world, the love of the Father is not in him. For all that is in the world, the lust of the flesh, and the lust of the eyes, and the pride of life, is not of the Father, but is of the world" (I John 2:15, 16).

In this connection let it be said emphatically that if God and His Christ occupy their proper place in our hearts there will be no room left for things worldly. If our appreciation and devotion to things spiritual is normal, the vain pleasures of sin and the friendship of the world will carry no appeal for us. Let us oppose worldly-mindedness most of all through the furtherance of a whole-hearted and God-centered Christianity!

It is not without reason that the Catechism mentions as sworn enemies of believers not only the devil and the world but also "our own flesh." In Holy Writ the word "flesh" often stands for the sinful desires of our hearts. Our natural depravity, as it continues to assert itself in the believer, is designated by this word "flesh." So, for instance, we read in Gal. 5:17: "For the flesh lusteth against the Spirit, and the Spirit against the flesh: and these are contrary the one to the other."

Now the devil and all the wicked demons of hell constitute a dreadful force against us; and the dangers to which we stand exposed day by day from the side of this sinful world is fearful indeed. But never should we forget the foe within the gates! Often the believer's greatest, most persistent and most subtle enemy is his own sinful heart! For without the heart the co-operation of the flesh, the devil and the world—no matter how great their power and influence—can accomplish nothing. This enemy, our own evil desire and inclination to sin, holds the key to the door through which the devil and the world gain admittance. The most godless radio program of jazz and nonsense will never reach you in your homes unless you have a receiving set—one that is in operation. Apart from our "flesh," Satan and the world would have no point of contact in our life. Yes, the devil is to blame. A fearful guilt is his. Words cannot express the greatness of his guilt for his monstrous activity as our tempter.

But his guilt does not in the least erase ours. Your responsibility for the sins which you have committed stands, my fellow-believer! You cannot clear yourself of guilt by pointing to the devil and the world of sin. For without your own consent to sin and love for sin, all the strength and ingenuity of the devil and all the allurements of the world would not in the least move you to sin. Remember this, and think of the words of Jeremiah: "The heart is deceitful above all things, and desperately wicked: who can know it?" (Jer. 17:9). Well may we pray with David: "Create in me a clean heart, O God; and renew a right spirit within me" (Ps. 51:10).

How much would we accomplish in our own strength against these sworn enemies of ours? Nothing! Our own depravity is so complete and our natural folly of heart and love for sin are so great that we stand ready to confess with Paul: "For I know that in me (that is, in my flesh) dwelleth no good thing: for to will is present with me; but how to perform that which is good I find not. For the good which I would I do not: but the evil which I would not, that I do" (Rom. 7:18, 19). And with that great apostle, excelling in grace and devotion, we exclaim upon due consideration: "Wretched man that I am! who shall deliver me from the body of this death?" (Rom. 7:24). We can only reply with him: "Jesus Christ!"

Well may we pray: "Be pleased to preserve and strengthen us by the power of Thy Holy Spirit, that we may not succumb in this spiritual warfare but always offer strong resistance, till at last we obtain a complete victory."

But in praying "Bring us not into temptation," we are virtually saying that God brings us into temptation. How is this to be understood? The devil tempts us. The world allures us. We walk into temptation and yield to its pull. But how can Jesus virtually say that His Father, the God of wondrous love and holiness, brings us, His children, into temptation?

Rest assured that God does not desire sin. His whole blessed being militates against it. Nor does He take a delight in any temptation on the part of the devil or his agencies. But God does lead His children into circumstances of life which expose them to the special attacks of the devil—not because He takes a delight in our exposure and yielding to sin, but because He would use the temptation to bless us, or to promote the cause of His kingdom. Thus it may be said that Adam and Eve were led into temptation by God. So also Job was brought into temptation through the sore afflictions which God permitted. Christ Himself was brought into temptation by God when the Spirit led Him into the wilderness to be tempted of Satan.

Now, Jesus teaches us to pray that we may be spared these fearful trials and conflicts; but that if in God's all-wise providence they must come, the Evil One may not succeed in his devilish attempts; that in the temptation we may be delivered from Satan and by the Holy Spirit gain the victory and so come forth out of the conflict triumphantly. And we may well say:

> Should Thy mercy send me
> Sorrow, toil, and woe,
> Or should pain attend me
> On my path below,
> Grant that I may never
> Fail Thy hand to see;
> Grant that I may ever
> Cast my care on Thee.

For indeed, God's ways are higher than ours, and His thoughts higher than our thoughts (Isa. 55:9). Again and again God's children must exclaim with the Psalmist: "Thy way, O God, is in the sanctuary" (Ps. 77:13). Remember this, children of God, when you are tempted by the Evil One in sickness and pain, when you stand at the open grave of your loved ones, or when grievous disappointments are yours.

God permits temptations and brings us into temptations, but always with a gracious purpose and from most holy motives: perhaps to test our loyalty and confidence in Him; perhaps to humble us when pride and self-confidence are harbored within; perhaps to demonstrate before men and angels the power of His grace in us; perhaps to strengthen and qualify us for more severe battles which await us; perhaps to enrich us spiritually that we may praise God the more, and encourage others in their trials and temptations. But whatever the temptation or whatever God's purpose, though often entirely hidden from our view, let us confidently assert:

> Oh, 'tis not in grief to harm me,
> While Thy love is left to me!

Upon this significant sixth petition follows the doxology: "For thine is the kingdom, and the power, and the glory for ever." This is a very brief but exultant hymn of praise.

When we go to God in prayer we go as His dear children, beloved of Him. As such we have experienced His loving care constantly and abundantly. It is altogether fitting, therefore, that we should conclude our prayers with a doxology of praise and confidence.

In this beautiful and dynamic conclusion to the Lord's Prayer, we first of all confess that God has the *authority* to grant our petitions. His is the Kingdom!

There is a Kingdom of God. The whole universe is its realm. All believers, those in heaven and those still on earth, together with all the holy angels, are its subjects. The Triune God is its sovereign King, ruling with absolute authority. And its future spells complete victory over sin and a glorious, eternal, heavenly harmony.

This kingdom is but partially in evidence upon this earth now. By God's permission sin is having its day, and Satan reigns in many hearts and homes—but only by God's permission. The kingdom *is* God's! God is King! Absolute King! Now! For Thine is the kingdom!"

This should comfort us.

When iniquity abounds in high places, even among civil rulers, let the child of God look up and say, "Thine is the kingdom!"

When business methods are corrupt and misrepresentations abound, to the disgust of Christian business men, look up and say: "Thine is the kingdom!"

When your employer withholds from you your just due, Christian employee, look up and say: "Thine is the kingdom!"

When life seems more like a devil's carnival than a well-ordered regime over which God rules; when sin seems stronger than righteousness; when pain and suffering and death seem to proclaim to you a Satanic reign of terror, look up and say: "Thine is the kingdom!"

Next, we confess that God has the *ability* to grant our petition: "Thine is the power."

God is the Almighty Creator, Ruler and Disposer of all things. God is *God,* which presupposes that supreme power is His. "Great is our Lord, and of great power," says the Psalmist (Ps. 147:5).

God is never helpless and impotent. What a comfort! Whenever we get what we did not desire, and fail to receive that for which we prayed, let us never even think of attributing inability to God. Almighty power is His!

Furthermore, he who uses this doxology aright thereby confesses that God has the *moral excellency* to answer our prayers. Thine is the glory! The word for glory which Christ uses in this doxology was often used for the Hebrew words that signify splendor and brightness. The glory of God, we may say, is His excellency. The glory of a diamond is its radiating luster. So the glory of God is the manifestation of His holiness, righteousness, love, faithfulness, omnipotence and all other excellencies of His being. God is good enough to grant our petitions. For His excellency exceeds all other excellency. We never need doubt His mercy and truth, His love and righteousness.

Let these facts be our abiding confidence. For God's authority, ability and excellency to grant our petitions, are eternal! He changes not. Forevermore let your reliance be on Him: in childhood and years of youth; in the full vigor of years and in old age; in joy and sorrow; in health and in sickness; in prosperity and in adversity; in life and in death. Then let also our adoration and praise be His forevermore!

This lofty doxology Christ concludes with the customary "Amen."

According to the significance of the word, "Amen" may mean: "We have prayed in sincerity and truthfulness," or, "May God hear our prayer"; or, "We have faith in God, that He will answer our prayer as is best"; or, "It shall truly and certainly be." The latter rendering is favored by our Catechism: ". . . for my prayer is more certainly heard of God than I feel in my heart that I desire these things of Him."

Glorious assurance, this!

Not always does God send an affirmative answer to our prayers by giving us just what we have desired. Sometimes the answer must be negative. But God always hears our prayers. And if compatible with our welfare, the coming of His kingdom and His own glory, He will give us our request. At all events He disposes of our prayers in all love and holiness and justice.

Let us confidently go to Him in prayer and conclude our petitions with an unfaltering "Amen" of faith.

For in the name of Him who is the Amen of God
(Rev. 3:14), we are eternally the objects of His bound-
less mercy!

> And blessed be His glorious Name,
> Long as the ages shall endure;
> O'er all the earth extend His fame.
> Amen, Amen, forevermore.